A BRIEF HISTORY
OF NORTHERN IRELAND

D1352284

SEAN McMAHON

THE BREHON PRESS
BELFAST

Published by
The Brehon Press Ltd,
19 Glen Crescent
Belfast BT11 8FB
Northern Ireland

ISBN: 978 1 905474 16 5

Printed in the EU

CONTENTS

Note: The term Nationalist (with an initial in upper case) refers only to members of the Nationalist Party. Otherwise the word is frequently used to describe non-Unionists.

The Welsh Wizard

ON 10 MARCH 1920 THE ENGLISH humorous magazine *Punch*, rarely a friend of Ireland, published a cartoon by its leading artist, Bernard Partridge (1861–1945), with the title 'The Welsh Wizard'. It showed David Lloyd George (1863–1945), then the British Prime Minister, cutting the map of Ireland in two, in fact estranging Ulster from the rest of the country. He is shown dropping the two pieces into a bag and saying (as the caption reads): 'After a suitable interval they will be found to come out together of their own accord – at least let's hope so. I've never done this trick before.' A fortnight before, the Conservatives with three times as many seats as Lloyd George's Liberals had determined that 'the area of Northern Ireland shall consist of the counties Antrim, Armagh, Down, Fermanagh, Londonderry and Tyrone and the parliamentary boroughs of Belfast and Londonderry'.

Lloyd George was known as the 'Welsh Wizard', partly because he was reared by his widowed Welsh mother and uncle in Criccieth, in north Wales, and partly because of his brilliant parliamentary career, which included the laying of the foundations of the welfare state by the establishing of national insurance and old age pensions, and also the weakening of the House of Lords veto. He was also the man who won the Great War. In 1920 he was the precarious leader of a coalition in danger of being toppled by Arthur Balfour (1848–1930), the leader of the Conservatives. He had a pretty shrewd idea that his conjuring was more a confidence trick than a piece of wizardry but he did not anticipate that his partitioning of Ireland and his treaty with Michael Collins (1890–1922), which established the Irish Free State, would so enrage the Conservatives that they effectively finished his political career.

He should have listened to his secretary of state for war, Winston Churchill (1873–1964), who never underestimated the complexity of Anglo-Irish relationships. Churchill's earliest years were spent in Ireland when his grandfather, the Duke of Marlborough, was viceroy (1876–80). As he reminded parliament on 16 February 1922, because of the war:

> The modes of thought of men, the whole outlook on affairs, the grouping of parties, all have encountered violent and tremendous changes in the deluge of the world. But as the deluge subsides and the waters fall short, we see the dreary steeples of Fermanagh and Tyrone emerging once again. The integrity of their quarrel is one of the few institutions that has been unaltered in the cataclysm which has swept the world.

Lloyd George was not the first British politician, nor would he be the last, to underestimate the intransigence of the northern Unionist and the admittedly more accommodating, but still intermittently abrasive, equivalent response from nationalists. What Louis MacNeice (1907–63) called 'the hard cold fire of the northerner' had persisted from the seventeenth century and to a certain extent still persists in the twenty-first.

When James I decided to impose 'civility' by planting Ulster with 'undertakers', English and Scots, he hoped for a kind of bloodless genocide; the dispossessed northern Irish would be scattered, isolated, and eventually become morally extinct. Two unfortunate facts prevented this: the foreigners could not impose civility without the labour of these dispossessed, and the same 'hard cold fire' enabled them to survive. The living conditions of the underclass were not all that different from those under the old Gaelic clan chieftains and they still had their dreams of a nobler life to buoy them up.

As the years passed the province became the home of two tribes not always in open war but never at peace. The anti-Planter uprising by Sir Phelim O'Neill in October 1641 hardened attitudes considerably. About a thousand Protestants were killed in Armagh, Antrim, Cavan and Fermanagh. That slaughter has never been forgotten and though casualties were grossly exaggerated, 1641 remains a time of infamy in Protestant folk memory as for others do the Great Famine in the nineteenth century and Pearl Harbor in the twentieth. As John Hewitt (1907–1987) wrote in his poem 'The Colony': 'That terror dogs us.'

Religion helped to unite the underprivileged Catholic native Irish, while Presbyterianism and, to a lesser extent, a fairly fundamentalist Anglicanism provided the moral authority of what the old Irish called the *Gall* – the foreigner. During the eighteenth century, well named the 'Protestant century', things were fairly quiet. At its end the United Irishmen stirred things up a bit but it was essentially a Presbyterian rising that did not involve Catholics much. Seventeen ninety-five, however, saw the founding of the Orange Order, an event that was to have a considerable negative effect on Catholics thereafter. They benefited, as did the rest of Ireland, from the political and educational advantages of emancipation but any attempt at Home Rule agitation was met with Orange rioting. When it seemed by 1912 that a limited autonomy might result, 474,414 people, of which 234,046 were women, signed the 'Solemn League and Covenant' against its implementation. They swore

> to stand by one another in defending for ourselves and our children our cherished position as equal citizenship in the United Kingdom, and in using all means which may be found necessary to defeat the conspiracy to set up a Home Rule Parliament in Ireland.

The signatories made up about half the total Protestant population of Ulster. In this oath they were merely echoing what Winston Churchill's father Lord Randolph had said on landing at Larne on 22 February 1886, when he proposed to play the Orange Card: 'Ulster at the proper moment will resort to its supreme arbitrament of force. Ulster will fight and Ulster will be right.' By September 1913 a provisional government with a military hierarchy was in existence and plans for a coup were in place.

The architects of this essentially treasonable activity were James Craig (1871–1940), the stolid but highly efficient son of a millionaire distiller, and member for East Down, and Sir Edward Carson (1854–1935), the brilliant barrister and MP for Dublin University, who had been knighted in 1900 and became head of the Unionist Party in 1910. It was he who nailed his irregular colours to the mast when at a rally in Coleraine on 21 September 1912 he announced that: 'In the event of this proposed parliament being thrust upon us, we solemnly and mutually pledge ourselves not to recognise its authority… I don't care whether it is treason or not.'

Whatever about his public utterances he tended to be more conciliatory in private. His purpose was the preservation of the union with Britain at all costs. To this end he and Craig set up the Ulster Volunteer Force (UVF) in January 1913. Though known as 'Carson's Army' its chief organiser was Craig and recruitment was mainly from Orange lodges throughout the nine counties, its membership reaching around 90,000 in 1914. Of these, 5,500, fighting as the 36th (Ulster) Division, and many of them wearing Orange collarettes, were killed at the Ancre river, a tributary of the Somme, on the 1st and 2nd of July 1916. This self-sacrifice was correctly seen as absolute proof of Ulster's unwavering support of the Union and in the months that followed (the Battle of the Somme lasted until 18 November) many more were killed. Their action has tended to be shown as being in sharp contrast to the 'stab in the back' of the Easter Rising, two months earlier. Yet, of a total of 50,000 Irish deaths in the

Great War, half at least were Catholic and presumed nationalist.

On the night of 24–25 April 1914, 25,000 rifles and one million rounds of ammunition were landed at Larne from the ship *Clyde Valley*. Smaller consignments arrived at Bangor and Donaghadee. They had been bought in Germany, Austria and Italy by Major F H Crawford, a Boer War veteran, for the UVF. The guns were transported to depots, usually Orange lodges, by car, and the smoothness of the operation provided evidence of Craig's organisational abilities, especially in the matter of mobilising the paramilitary force. It was more of a political success than a military achievement because of the relative paucity of ammunition and the complexity of the weapons but it showed that if necessary Ulster *would* fight. The 'Curragh Incident' a month earlier, in which Major-General Hubert Gough persuaded fifty-seven out of seventy officers of the regular army to state that they would resign rather than move against opponents of Home Rule, had shown that the Liberal War Office had little control over the army. It is clear that Carson and Craig were kept informed of all developments by members of the High Command. Unionist Ulster was more than ready for an armed struggle; with typical efficiency plans for evacuating civilians and designs for an Ulster currency had already been approved.

H H Asquith (1852–1928), the Liberal Prime Minister, was forced to compromise in his Home Rule bill. The means of allowing individual counties to opt out of the terms of the law was included in the revised bill. The opt-out clause was to allow a temporary exclusion on a county basis for six years. Carson's response was: 'We do not want a sentence of death with a stay of execution for six years.' The Lords successfully emended it to allow nine unspecified counties to disregard the measure permanently.

George V (1865–1936), assumed to be on the side of the Ulster 'disloyalists', called a conference in Buckingham Palace of Unionist and Nationalist representatives on 21 July 1914 in an attempt to break the impasse over Home Rule. The king said in his opening speech: 'We have watched with deep misgivings the course of events in Ireland… To me it is unthinkable, as it must be to you, that we should be brought to the brink of fratricidal strife upon issues apparently so capable of adjustment.' They were fine words but totally ineffective. The conference broke up on 24 July without any settlement. As Asquith described it afterwards: 'Nothing could have been more amicable in tone or more desperately fruitless in result.'

It was clear by then that Lloyd George, though still only Chancellor of the Exchequer, was the real power in the cabinet and that he intended to impose a settlement involving some degree of separation for the Unionists. In the first week of August, Germany invaded neutral Belgium and declared war on France on the third of that month. The next day Britain responded by declaring war on Germany, ironically the source of most of the UVF guns. Agitation about Ulster was shelved 'until the end of hostilities' but its future had already been decided by the impatient and ruthless Lloyd George. Derry, Antrim, Down and Armagh – the predominantly Protestant counties – were going to be part of a region that would not be governed by Dublin. What was unclear was the fate of Derry City, Tyrone, Fermanagh, Donegal, Cavan and Monaghan.

In 1918 Carson, who had served in several ministerial capacities and was a member of the war cabinet, resigned. Always a paradoxical figure – he said that the one affection left to him was his love of Ireland – his fulminations against Home Rule sounded slightly dissonant in a strong Dublin accent. He was the most literal Unionist of them all, fighting to maintain Ireland in the United Kingdom and deeply opposed to partition. Craig, knighted in 1918 for services during the war, was more pragmatic. If partition would result in the permanent hegemony of Unionism and the permanent exclusion from power of nationalists then he would most gratefully accept it.

Carson might have accepted a separate state comprising the nine counties of the historical province of Ulster, and that arrangement would have pleased Lloyd George and the British government as it was likely, with its approximately equal numbers of Catholics and Protestants, to lead to unification with the other three provinces. It had been clear, however, from the end of the Easter Rising in 1916 that even the Irish Parliamentary Party had acquiesced in the notion of a separate six-county state. The idea was greatly deplored by northern nationalists; at a protest meeting on 20 July 1916 a letter was read out from Charles McHugh (1855–1926), the fiery Catholic Bishop of Derry. In it he condemned 'the nefarious scheme' of Lloyd George:

> What seems to be the worst feature of all this wretched bargaining is that Irishmen, calling themselves representatives of the people, are prepared to sell their brother Irishmen into slavery to secure a nominal freedom for a section of the people... Was coercion of a more objectionable or despicable type ever resorted to by England in its dealings with Ireland than that now sanctioned by the men whom we elected to win us freedom?

The Irish Situation Committee, chaired by the pro-Unionist Walter Long (1854–1924), reported on 4 November 1919 and its findings became the basis for the Government of Ireland Act. Long had been instrumental in blocking Lloyd George's initiative of giving Home Rule to twenty-six counties immediately after the Easter Rising and now he made the Northern Ireland state a fact. His original suggestion was that the separate state comprise the nine counties of the historical province of Ulster but Balfour, strongly motivated by Craig's insistence that he could not govern Donegal, Cavan and Monaghan, demanded from Lloyd George that these problematic counties should be excluded.

There was always going to be a difficulty about naming the separated part of Ireland. The preferred 'Ulster' was simply inaccurate, geographically and historically; Northern Ireland was no more accurate. It was a commonly heard and wearisomely repeated joke in Derry in the 1930s that people heading to Inishowen, the most northerly part of Donegal, would say, 'We're going south politically but north geographically.' Nationalists simply referred to it dismissively as the 'Six Counties' and devised the acronym 'Fatdad' to represent Fermanagh, Antrim, Tyrone, Derry, Armagh and Down. For Unionists the acronym became 'Fatlad', calling the north-western county by the historically more accurate title of Londonderry. Even after the coming of the border the *Derry Journal*, the leading nationalist organ in the northwest, never referred to the inaccurately titled 'Ulster' without quotation marks, even calling the bus transport authority 'U'TA and the local commercial television station 'U'TV.

Though not a man to win ready sympathy one cannot help feeling a little sorry for the Welsh Wizard in the circumstances. He had the reputation of being too clever by half and, though Welsh, had no sympathy with Irish separatist ambitions. He, like his Liberal predecessors, would dearly love to have found the answer to the Irish Question. He might have done wonders if he had not been distracted by the coming of the terrible war. Though urged by Asquith to impose Home Rule in 1916 he was balked by Long and had little heart in the apparently rash act. With such slaughter among the young men of Europe he wished that at least the Irish settlement should be bloodless. As a successful Welshman who felt little sense of English tyranny he found it hard to understand why the Irish should feel such a sense of wrong at the persistence of the Union. Wales had lost little, he felt, by its sixteenth-century linking with England. His lack of realisation of the difference between the original colonisation of Ireland and that of his own country gave him a kind of tunnel vision. One cannot imagine that with his temperament he would have found much common psychological ground with the Unionists of Ulster. He was, however, persuaded of their realistic fears by Carson and probably believed that Home Rule would lead to 'Rome Rule'. He lived to see some evidence of strong Catholic Church influence in the Free State that he had created.

It was not so much because of Lloyd George's pro-Unionist bias that he was execrated by nationalists north and south. It was rather because, impatient with the Irish Republican Army (IRA) and euphoric at his successful prosecution of the Great War, he sent in the hated and violent Black and Tans in January 1920 to defeat them in the Anglo-Irish war.[1] In spite of the fearsomeness of this irregular force it did not defeat the IRA. Chagrined at the bloody stalemate Lloyd George was adamant about the strict application of the treaty terms and must take some of the responsibility for the civil war which broke out in Ireland in June 1922.[2] His solution of the problem, the Government of Ireland Act (1920), gave the Unionists what they wanted and left nationalists with only thirteen sixteenths of what they wanted. A pragmatic politician at all times, he knew that the Unionists, with the resurrected and well-armed UVF, and their strong support from the Conservatives, could prove a greater threat to civic order than the IRA.

The act that became law nine months after the Welsh Wizard cartoon appeared in *Punch* had the optimistic title of 'Act for the Better Government of Ireland'. It suited the Unionists, if no one else. Because of their history, which included a fleeting sense of guilt about what their ancestors had agreed to do, they remained watchful. Some commentators referred to their mindset perhaps too strongly as 'siege mentality' but they were constantly vigilant and permanently distrustful of the majority Irish Catholics. Only in Ulster had Protestants a two-thirds majority. John Hewitt summed up the guilt and the wariness in the poem 'The Colony', quoted earlier, 'We took the kindlier soils…', and later, 'Teams of the tamer natives we employed/to hew and draw, but we did not call them slaves.' Watchfulness became endemic and though for most of the time relations between the two tribes were nearly amicable, there could never be trust. It galled the Protestants of Derry – an historical name of the city that even they used for convenience in conversation – that, because of the Great Famine of the 1840s and the natural magnetic appeal of an urban centre, their city should have a majority of *them*. The Maiden City that had withstood the famous siege had been infiltrated. Though there was never a majority in Belfast there was a minority increasing steadily because of perceived 'animal-like' breeding.

The hatred and fear of the Roman Catholic Church – its 'Italian' allegiance never forgotten – was a constant preoccupation. The dread of 'Rome Rule' under a Home Rule Ireland was exacerbated by the ill-timed *Ne Temere* decree promulgated by Pius X (1835–1914) in 1908 that insisted that children of a mixed marriage be reared as Catholics. Though merely a reaffirmation of long-standing church teaching its effect in the Ireland of the time seemed to confirm a perceived growth in ecclesiastic power and showed little charity to Protestants.

Another mark of distinction was Unionists' pride in their Britishness and a loyalty to the empire that was even then beginning to fray at the edges. Implicit too in the attitudes personalised in Craig, though probably not in Carson, was the need to assume a moral superiority over what Kipling, in a not entirely different context, called 'the lesser breeds without the law'. In the circumstances it would have taken heroic courage and confidence on Lloyd George's part to insist on acceptance of an all-Ireland system.

Though it savours a little of wilder conspiracy theory one cannot exculpate the Conservative Party of the time entirely from the charge of deliberately manipulating Craig and his Unionists to regain power after years of Liberal supremacy. It was why Lord Randolph Churchill decided, if necessary, to play the Orange Card in 1886. As he wrote to Lord Justice Fitzgibbon on 16 February of that year: 'I decided some time ago that if the GOM ['Grand Old Man', i.e. Gladstone] went for Home Rule, the Orange Card would be the one to play. Please God it may be the ace of trumps and not the two.' The playing of the card was not necessary then because the once Liberal Joseph Chamberlain seceded from the party to form the 'Unionist' Party.

Now, with Balfour's Conservatives breathing down his neck, and not entirely to defend the empire, Lloyd George decided to settle for his 'trick' with consequences still with us today. The creation of the Northern Ireland state was a kind of final smack in the face for those who made the first attack on the empire. If the British government of the time could have realised just what a drain on the exchequer the excised counties would constitute for the next fifty years they might not have been so sanguine about standing by their Unionist brothers. It was a time when extremist elements were in the ascendancy. Relations between Catholics and Protestants had been for the most part reasonable. The minuscule Catholic middle class, merchants, doctors and lawyers with an almost exclusive confessional clientele, and clerics, on the whole, lived in polite amity with Protestant neighbours. The Catholic working class, though showing a greater level of unemployment than their Protestant brothers, had, because of the war, done quite well. Now in peacetime, returning ex-servicemen demanded reinstatement.

In the summer of 1920 more than 1,000 Catholic employees had been ousted from their jobs in Belfast. Some of the worst violence was witnessed in the 'Island', the site of Belfast's famous shipbuilding industry. On 21 July 'disloyal' Catholics were driven out, some thrown into the river and having to swim ashore. In the three days of rioting that followed seven Catholics and six Protestants were killed. On 14 October, Craig visited the shipyard and addressed the now exclusively Protestant workers: 'Do I approve of the action you boys have taken in the past? I say yes.'

The trouble may have been partly engendered by the news from Derry, where serious rioting had started on 19 July. A nationalist parade involving Sinn Féin and supporters of the Irish Party was not allowed to march around the storied city walls, a privilege reserved for the Apprentice Boys of Derry who had just made that circuit on the 'Twelfth' to celebrate the ending of the iconic siege of 1688–9.[3] The serious rioting that followed included looting.

The following January, under the Proportional Representation (PR) system, Derry, with a Catholic majority of 5,000, had in a solicitor, H C O'Doherty, its first Catholic mayor by a margin of one in the Corporation. A forgivable euphoria in O'Doherty's first public speeches was interpreted as triumphalism and was said to have raised fears in the Protestant population. Some of his remarks were not unexpected but hardly judicious in the prevailing climate. As reported by the *Derry Journal* of 20 January, the new mayor said, 'Ireland's right to determine her own destiny will come about whether the Protestants of Ulster like it or not.' Such enthusiasm combined with the ceasing of the flying of the Union flag increased local tension.[4]

The mayoral election coincided with some low-level IRA activity but things were generally quiet, if tense, until April 1920. The Derry Jail, built in 1791 and turreted in 1824, was located in Bishop Street Without the Walls. It was at the city gate here that James II had been met with a defiant 'No surrender' on 18 April 1689, and the part of the street that held the jail was for about 300 yards a neutral boundary between the Protestant Fountain area and the Catholic Bogside. In its time the jail had held a rich variety of convicts, including Patrick Gallagher (1871–1964), better known as 'Paddy the Cope', the founder of the Templecrone Cooperative Society, and Louis J Walsh (1880–1942), later District Justice in Donegal, the author of the Ulster comedy *The Pope in Killybuck* (1915). Now it held internees from the IRA. Rioting started when, on 14 April, IRA prisoners arrived for incarceration and opposing groups faced each other on the Bishop Street interface. Shots were fired, almost certainly by UVF guns stored since April 1914, into the Bogside. It was the first of many examples of serious civic unrest that lasted for most of the summer, being particularly violent at weekends.

At 10.30am on 15 May a riot began at Ferryquay Gate, the scene of the London apprentices' defiance in 1688. Carlisle Road was, like Bishop Street Without, a place of confrontation between Catholics and Protestants. The other end of Fountain Street faced Bridge Street, a working class Catholic area. As was to be the custom for the next half-century it was nationalists that the police charged rather than their adversaries, driving them down to the river's edge on the quay with fixed bayonets. Some members of the crowd fired revolvers at the police while they scattered. Reaching that part of the quay near the Great Northern Railway station they continued to fire from behind railway wagons. The only casualty was DS Denis Moroney, head of the CID in the city, who was shot shortly after reaching the river. He was carried to the Metropole Hotel at the foot of Bridge Street, where he died from his wounds. A native of County Clare, Moroney was the first member of the Royal Irish Constabulary (RIC) to be killed in the North during the Troubles. The first Catholic to be killed was an ex-soldier called Bernard O'Doherty, who was hit by a sniper's bullet in Orchard Street, that runs from Foyle Street up to the Carlisle Road interface.

On Sunday, 13 June Catholics walking in Prehen Wood on the east bank of the Foyle were attacked by Protestants. The incident was regarded as minor since there were no fatalities but the following Friday there was rioting, shooting and looting on the same side of the river in the Waterside area of the city. This was followed late on the Saturday night by a serious gunfight in which several Catholics were killed. The flashpoint was just outside Bishop Gate, and began as a fight among drunks. The IRA tried to occupy the part of the city within the old walls but they were driven out by the UVF which had superior gun power. The IRA retreated down Bishop Street Without and occupied St Columb's College, perhaps with the encouragement of Bishop McHugh who lived there. The building was empty of any pupils because the dayboys and boarders were at home on the long summer vacation. The UVF occupied the Horsemarket at the top of Abercorn Road that runs from the Craigavon Bridge to Bishop Street Without. Throughout the night of Tuesday, 22 June and into the Wednesday morning the college was raked by UVF fire. The *Derry Journal* of Friday, 25 June reported:

> In consequence of the regular sniping at St Columb's College from the Unionists in Barrack Street, Old Horse Market, and adjoining streets, here for the first time since the Unionist outburst, the Irish Volunteers have entered into the awful fray. They replied effectively to the fire from the Unionist quarters. So heavy was the barrage maintained on some streets that the Unionists were unable to move out and were obliged to remain under shelter all night.

The battles raged for a week with an estimated forty deaths, a majority of them not reported to the authorities. By Saturday, 26 June a sufficient number of extra soldiers had arrived in the city to be able to declare martial law and impose a strict curfew from 11pm till 5am. This was made even more stringent the following April when the curfew began at 9.30pm.

The difficulty of carrying on a normal social life under these conditions gave rise to many Derry myths and oft-told tales sprinkled with a deal of local humour. The instinct for carrying on in spite of bullets and other aspects of the terror was reassuringly demonstrated on the black day of 20 June. On that Sunday the evening *paseo* of young men and women that usually paraded down Carlisle Road, across the Carlisle Bridge (the Craigavon Bridge's predecessor), and out along the Prehen Road by the Foyle continued as usual but in safer parts of the town. Those who were young at the time, telling the story later, said the army turned the guns on both sides and achieved a sort of peace. This was not quite the case; the army's instincts for survival had it cooperate visibly with the UVF as the stronger side. The Dorset regiment discovered an affinity with them and the RIC seemed to the perhaps prejudiced eyes of Derry nationalists, both moderates and IRA, to be extremely partial in their tactics. There were regular complaints that after rioting it was only in Catholic areas that arms searches were made.

The UVF had shown that they had much superior firepower and, apart from actions by a few individuals, the IRA did very little in the city. There had never been much of a presence there; members were generally older and showed a reluctance, not shared by the south Derry brigade or the east Donegal contingent, to kill fellow Irishmen even when wearing RIC uniforms. One cogent reason for the general inactivity, apart from awareness of the armed superiority of the enemy, was the fact that the clergy, led by Bishop McHugh, had reasserted their pastoral control over the city. This was made possible by the command disarray and internal squabbling among IRA members. This strong clerical influence was to continue after the passing of the partitioning act and set the pattern, for better or worse, of Catholic response to the new dispensation.

In a sense, events in Derry, though bloody and probably deliberately organised to show that a Catholic mayor did not mean a Catholic city, were a sideshow; Belfast and Lisburn were scenes of much greater violence. Derry, however, was from a Unionist standpoint still the Maiden City. Its iconic strength was based upon its glorious history in Protestant eyes. As the city's laureate, Charlotte Elizabeth Tonna (1790–1846), had written about the original apprentices' response to Lord Antrim:

> They shouted 'No Surrender!'
>   And slammed it in his face.
> Then, in a quiet tone, boys,
>   They told him 'twas their will
> That the Maiden on her throne, boys,
>   Should be a Maiden still.

The Unionists needed the siege city as a prize and were determined to have it as a part of their separate identity. Its loyalty had to be clear and unequivocal and its citizens' compliance was a necessary part of their future.

21

The (Better) Government of Ireland Act

THE FIRST PART OF THE WELSH Wizard's conjuring trick was the Better Government of Ireland Act that was introduced into parliament on 25 February 1920 and became law on 23 December. The use of the word 'better' in the title seemed somehow to expect the question: better than what?

It proposed two parliaments for Ireland, one to handle the affairs of twenty-six counties, meeting in Dublin, the other to rule the six north-eastern counties of 'Fatlad' with Belfast as its capital and 'the city of Londonderry' included more for myth than good measure. Carson had not wanted any erosion in the Union but had observed that Derry, Antrim, Down and Armagh would constitute a viable unit with a population greater than that of New Zealand or Newfoundland, and, though he did not say it, without the possible difficulty of dealing with Tyrone and Fermanagh with their majority of nationalists. Sir James Craig achieved his goal largely with the assistance of Balfour. In the general election of 24 May 1921, 124 Sinn Féin candidates were returned unopposed to the Southern parliament but they boycotted the first meeting, which was attended by four Unionists elected for Trinity. The results in Northern Ireland had Unionists 40, Sinn Féin 6, Irish Party 6. The large overall

Unionist majority was to be maintained for fifty-one years until Edward Heath's announcement on 24 March 1972 of the suspension of the Stormont government and its replacement by direct rule with William Whitelaw (1918–99) as the first Secretary of State for Northern Ireland.

The first Northern Ireland parliament met on 7 June in the ostentatious City Hall, now in its fifteenth marbled year, and Craig was elected Prime Minister. It received more than formal assent with its state opening on 22 June by George V. The king took the opportunity in another speech of late-blossoming statesmanship of pleading for reconciliation between the communities. Though meant sincerely it could not help sounding hollow, especially to the beleaguered Catholics who had suffered so much in the city for the previous twelve months:

> I speak from a full heart when I pray that my coming to Ireland today may prove to be first step towards an end of strife among her people, whatever their race or creed. In that hope I appeal to all Irishmen to pause to stretch out the hand of forbearance and conciliation, to forgive and forget, and to join in making for the land that they love a new era of peace, contentment and goodwill... May this historic gathering be the prelude of a day in which the Irish people, North and South, under one parliament or two, as those parliaments may themselves decide, shall work together in common love for Ireland upon the sure foundation of mutual justice and respect.

Clearly the king believed that the partition of the country would be as temporary as his government assured him it would be. Though what he uttered seemed to nationalists 'polite meaningless words', they were well-intentioned and may have been one thin strand in the fabric that led to the Truce between the IRA and the British authorities that followed on 11 July.

The year of the progress of the 'better act' had been bloody as no other year in the century so far. It took little to inflame the sectarian North. As noted earlier, 21 July, the first working day after the

'Twelfth' holiday saw the expulsion of Catholic workers from the shipyard. The speeches made at various Orange venues had helped to raise tensions, especially one by Carson at the 'Field' at Finaghy, announcing, 'We in Ulster will tolerate no Sinn Féin.' Mob logic had no difficulty in deciding that all Catholics were, if not members of that organisation, then fervid supporters of it. The twenty-first of July was also the day of the funeral of Lt-Col G F Smyth DSO (1885–1920), Divisional Police Commissioner for Munster. One-armed because of a wound suffered in October 1914 with the British Expeditionary Force in France, he had issued a number of orders to his division of the RIC that seemed to suggest a 'shoot-on-sight' policy. His remarks to the RIC members in Listowel, County Kerry were deemed so inflammatory that one constable, Jeremiah Mee, removed his revolver and placed it on the table in front of Smyth, saying that he would no longer serve. Ordered to remove him the other constables refused. News of this 'Listowel mutiny' spread rapidly and Smyth was identified by the IRA as a significant threat, a dangerous opponent. He was shot by a party of the No. 1 Brigade of the Cork IRA on 17 July in the smoking room of the Country Club in Cork City.

The death of Smyth brought the war that was being fought in the south uncomfortably close to Belfast. He was buried in the family plot in Banbridge and that evening Catholic businesses and houses in the town were attacked by loyalists. There was also trouble in Dromore, seven miles away. Over the next few days Catholics were literally driven out of both towns. There was also trouble in Bangor but Belfast, as ever, bore the brunt. It was to be the scene of recurring sectarian conflict over the next two years. In that time 453 people were killed; of these thirty-seven were members of the security forces and the rest civilians, 257 Catholics and 159 Protestants. More than 10,000 Catholics were driven from their jobs and 23,000 (a quarter of the total number in the city) were forced to flee their homes. One of those evicted from north Belfast was J[ames] J[oseph]

Campbell (1910–79), later Director of the Institute of Education at Queen's. In the 1940s while head of Classics at St Malachy's College, his old school, he published a series of articles in the *Capuchin Annual*, under the pen-name *Ultach* ('Ulsterman') and afterwards collected as *Orange Terror* in 1943. It was a coldly effective and unanswerable indictment of the Stormont regime's treatment of Catholics and it went unanswered. Five hundred Catholic businesses were destroyed. The Russian word *pogrom*, meaning 'lynching', and used to describe the Cossacks' murderous attacks on Russian Jews, seemed appropriate to describe the treatment of Belfast Catholics.[1]

Many of those carrying out the killings, sometimes admittedly defensive, were members of the UVF, now given ultra-respectability as the Ulster Special Constabulary (USC) that came into existence in November 1920. It was another demand of Craig's that the British government assented to with little reluctance. Belfast people knew what its existence would mean. Joseph ('Wee Joe') Devlin (1871–1934), the charismatic MP for West Belfast, made the position abundantly clear during the Commons debates on 25 October:

> The Chief Secretary is going to arm pogromists to murder Catholics… The Protestants are to be armed, for we would not touch your special constabulary with a forty-foot pole. The pogrom is to be made less difficult. Instead of paving stones and sticks, they are to given rifles.

Devlin was the darling of Belfast Catholics. He had beaten de Valera in the 1918 election and later served both in Westminster and the Northern Ireland Parliament. Dubbed by Tim Healy (1855–1931), the first Governor-General of Saorstát Éireann (during whose term of office Áras an Uachtaráin was known as 'Uncle Tim's Cabin'), the 'Duodecimo Demonsthenes', because of his small stature and oratorical brilliance, his whole political career was spent in tireless defence of his people.[2] Later, opposing the third reading of the partition bill on 11 November, he summed up nationalist fears:

> They take the Catholic minority... and place that minority at the mercy of the Protestant majority, and they plead in the most tender way, almost with tears in their voice, for the acceptance of this Bill, that it may end religious rancour... my friends and myself, 340,000 Catholics... are to be left permanently and enduringly at the mercy of the Protestant Parliament in the North of Ireland.

There were to be four categories of special constable: 2,000 A-specials, who would be full-time, mobile and uniformed and paid like the RIC; 19,500 B-specials, who would be part-time, uniformed and unpaid, and who could be armed from stores in police barracks; C-specials, who were older and a reserve to be used only in dire emergencies; and a short-lived force of C1-specials, who were rather like the British Territorial Army (TA). The A-specials were disbanded in 1926 and the C groups even earlier. The B-specials remained as the particular bane of Catholics, mobilised during the marching season, acting as a kind of Home Guard during the Second World War, and used as border patrols during the IRA campaign of 1956–62. The original rule about keeping their rifles in police barracks stores for issue was soon dropped as the violence in 1922 seemed endless, and the B-men were allowed to keep their rifles at home. Their partial and undisciplined behaviour during the civil rights movement and the charge that the Tynan (County Tyrone) corps had been guilty of a civilian death in August 1969 led to their disbandment in 1970. Recruitment was open to Catholics but some county commanders refused to accept them and there was no drive to allow Catholics to carry legal arms. The B-specials were in the end a totally sectarian force, recruited mainly from the UVF, and containing convicted criminals. Some of their members had earlier been in the United Protestant League (UPL), a notorious anti-Catholic murder gang.

Permission to form these constabularies had been granted 'to keep the King's peace'. In the climate of the time senior Unionist politicians were given more or less what they demanded. The

Conservative majority in the coalition government at Westminster was only too pleased to help their loyalist brothers who were defending the Empire that was being effectively attacked outside of Ulster. Though IRA activity in the north was muted compared with that in the other three provinces there were security force casualties. In the year 1920 eight RIC officers, including a head-constable, were shot at various locations in Northern Ireland, including two in Derry, one in Belfast, and one in Newry. The most sensational of these killings was that of District Inspector Oswald Swanzy in Lisburn on Sunday, 22 August. Swanzy was believed to have led the party that shot Tomas MacCurtain, Lord Mayor of Cork, and leader of the IRA in the city, on 20 March. He was named by the coroner's jury as one of the perpetrators. He was transferred out of Cork and Michael Collins, using one of his contacts in the RIC, traced him to Lisburn. His burial led to three days of rioting in Lisburn and Belfast. In Lisburn sixty public houses and shops owned by Catholics were set on fire as was the parish priest's house. Most of Lisburn's Catholics were driven out, taking refuge in Dundalk. In Belfast twenty-two people were killed and small Catholic ghettos in Protestant areas, such as the 'Bone' between Ardoyne and the Old Park Road, the streets that led from the Falls Road to the Shankill, and St Matthew's parish in Ballymacarrett, where the church and convent were virtually besieged for more than two years, were attacked.

Craig and Carson remained unmoved by the violence and made no effort to assist beleaguered Catholics. Their intention was clearly to establish Protestant supremacy and to show by implication what life would be like for 'Shinners' in the new state. The fact that not all working class Belfast Catholics, and few of the middle class, supported IRA activities was ignored. It was convenient for the authorities to regard all non-loyalists as the enemy. If they were uncomfortable about the north's international reputation they bore their discomfort well. Craig responded to pressure from Lloyd George by threatening to resign.[3] After the slaughter of the trenches life was held to be cheap and, though the greater number of killings was of Catholics, innocent Protestants suffered too.

One reason for Lloyd George's assent to the establishment of the USC was that, unsuitable as many of its members were, he felt it better that they have a quasi-official status with the implicit sanction of military discipline rather than have them act as freelance vigilantes. Cynics might say that that was precisely what they were – but in uniform. The IRA did not help by continuing actions that led to retaliation on any convenient northern Catholics. A boycott on Belfast goods imposed by Dublin and maintained during the Irish Civil War by the anti-Treatyites did little to improve the condition of Catholics and increased the economic distress that they were suffering.

Belfast celebrated the truce of 11 July, which meant essentially that the IRA had won the Anglo–Irish war, for them the War of Independence, in a not unexpected way. The following excerpt from a letter written the following day by a woman resident of Mulholland Terrace in the Falls Road described the events of the weekend:

> Yes we had a night and day of terror in the City on Sat. and Sunday; all day after 12 o'c. On Saturday night a car of Sp–cls came down the Terrace guns up and singing at a high pitch at the convent wall; they fired shot after shot & I hope no-one on the earth except the Sp–cls and their colleagues will ever experience such a night of terror, but thank God they met their match before daybreak; it was a continuous night of shooting, sometimes we lay flat on the ground, the firing was so near; if it was not for the boys in the locality we would have had the fate of Cupar St., our houses burned over us… Notwithstanding all this and their past year's work, the Orange procession walked up the Broadway Rd. out onto the Falls & down Thames Street with their sashes and drums & of course R.I.C. protection but there is none for Catholic property or life at this time of danger as you see by the paper.

It is interesting to note that even a respectable middle class Catholic could not but rejoice that the 'Sp–cls' had 'met their match'. In the week of 9–15 July the riots in Ballymacarrett were responsible for sixteen deaths, sixty-eight life-threatening injuries and the inevitable destruction of Catholic property and businesses. There was rioting again in August when twenty deaths were recorded in the north of the city. In September troops fired on Protestant rioters in York Street, killing two women; on 24 September a youth was shot dead leaving St Matthew's Church in the Catholic Short Strand area; the following day a bomb thrown by a Catholic in Seaforde Street in the same area killed two people, and a Protestant response in the now-vanished Weaver Street killed a man and seriously injured four children under six years of age. Some days later Catholics firing at a Protestant funeral killed one mourner. Rioting that month caused twenty-seven deaths and, by the end of 1921, the total number of killings was 109.

The first special constable to die was Robert William Compston. He was part of an escort of five who protected a postman as he did his rounds between Crossmaglen and Cullyhanna on 13 January 1921. They were ambushed by about fifty men at a sharp bend in the road and Compston, a twenty-four-year old man from Whitecross, County Armagh, was killed. The postman, who was shot in the back, died that day from his wounds. In all, ten specials died in 1921 and twenty-three in 1922. The tally of RIC/RUC casualties kept pace. In 1921 and 1922 a total of twenty officers were killed, eleven of them in Belfast.

It was the killing of the male members of the McMahon family on 24 March 1922, however, that shocked even those most hardened to the cruelty of the times. Two specials had been killed the day before and that was used as the excuse for the atrocity. William Chermside from Portaferry and Thomas Cunningham from County Cavan were on foot patrol in Victoria Street and were turning into May Street when an IRA group fired a number of shots at them; both died from their wounds. The killers were anti-Treatyites and in some misguided way must have felt that continuing to shoot policemen was part of their duty.

Early next morning the home of Owen McMahon, a wealthy Catholic publican who owned several Belfast bars, the largest of them in Ann Street in the city centre, was attacked. The house, in Kinnaird Terrace, off the lower Antrim Road, was broken into by a number of armed men, reportedly in 'police uniform'. The male members of the family – Frank, Patrick, Thomas, Owen, John and Bernard – and a bartender called Edward McKinney were dragged out of their beds and lined up against the wall of the dining-room. Twelve shots were fired; Frank, Patrick, Thomas, and McKinney died immediately; the father and Bernard died later in the Mater hospital. Apart from Owen, who was fifty years old, and Thomas, who was fifteen and a half, the men were in their early twenties. A child of six had escaped death by diving under a sofa and, though two shots were fired at it, he was not hit. Even the *Belfast News Letter*, strongly Unionist in sympathy, called it a 'detestable crime'. The raiders were almost certainly led by District Inspector J W Nixon, who was dismissed from the force in 1924 but lived to become an extremist independent Unionist for Woodvale (1929–49). No one was ever brought to justice for the outrage and Catholics had their worst fears realised.

The pages of the nationalist papers of the period make grim reading. In its coverage of the McMahon atrocity the *Derry Journal* of Monday, 27 March, revealed that the surviving sons, John and Michael, insisted that the murderers were in uniform and spoke with pronounced Belfast accents, as they said before opening fire, 'Well, boys, do you say any prayers?' The paper quoted the Dublin *Freeman's Journal*, comparing the massacre to that of Dolly's Brae, a Catholic district near Castlewellan, County Down, on 12 July 1849, when thirty Catholics were killed by Orangemen returning from Newcastle and escorted by troops. Over previous months the *Derry Journal* had recounted many examples of Catholic deaths about the province. One miserable story in the edition of Friday, 24 February, described how fifty ex-servicemen were evicted from

Craigavon, once Craig's house, but now a hospital for those suffering from shellshock, by members of the Orange Order, who left a note that ended with the sentence:

> Time is up: go or we will riddle every rotten Papish in Craigavon, as you are a right lot of————

The *Journal* was too decorous a paper to print the last word. As a potent and cheering indication that everyday life continues in spite of turmoil, the same edition of the paper that described the harrowing scenes at the McMahon funerals also announced that the cinema in St Columb's Hall would begin the first episode of a new serial, *The Count of Monte Cristo*.

In that month of March 1922 a total of sixty-one people were killed. There had been trouble in February when twenty-seven people died and sixty-eight were seriously wounded. On 17 April rioting in the 'Bone' resulted in the deaths of a Catholic and a Protestant. The result was the all-too-familiar burning of fifty Catholic homes in Saunderson Street and Antiqua Street in the Ardoyne district.

The IRA continued its campaign of attacking police, taking over barracks, and burning flax mills. They seemed oblivious of the reprisals that their enthusiastic 'armed struggle' was having on Catholics. The IRA itself was in turmoil, having to decide whether to accept the terms of the Treaty that had been signed on 6 December 1921. Collins did what he could for northern Catholics though he had other priorities of much greater concern with the setting up of the new Free State and having to deal with a brewing civil war begun by old comrades who would not accept the settlement. In an attempt to drive Craig to do something about the slaughter of Catholics, especially in Belfast, he made an official pact with him in London on 30 March 1922. Craig agreed to recruit Catholics for the USC and reinstate Catholics in their jobs in the shipyards, while Collins promised to prevent IRA intrusion from the twenty-six counties. Neither side kept the terms of the pact and the months of May and

June 1922 were among the worst of the current violence. Even the *Irish News*, then as now the voice of moderate nationalism, called upon the IRA extremists to stop their campaign since it was ultimately Catholics and not Unionists who suffered. In fact, as in Derry the previous year, by the end of July the IRA was a spent force.

With characteristic, if unimaginative, efficiency, Craig had his cabinet chosen by the end of May in 1921, a mere week after his unsurprising majority of forty Unionists to six Nationalists (as the Irish Party now called themselves) and six Sinn Féin. It was to be a result that would show little numerical change for the next fifty years. Essentially a man who disliked extremism in spite of his reputation with Catholics, his appointments were largely of worthy men with little talent. No bright young men had yet surfaced out of the murky soup of his militant supporters. John Miller Andrews (1871–1956), a linen and rope manufacturer, was Minister of Labour (1921–1937) and later Craig's successor as Prime Minister (1940–3); Hugh McDowell Pollock (1852–1937), who later became unpopular for his belief that Northern Ireland should be self-supporting, became Minister of Finance; Edward Mervyn Archdale (1853–1943) from Fermanagh undertook Agriculture and Commerce; and Education was given to Charles Stewart Henry Vane-Tempest Stewart, 7th Marquis of Londonderry (1878–1949), one of the richest men in what was then called without hesitation the British Isles, and who owned much of County Down. These men served the new state well even if the style of Londonderry was rather too flamboyant for fustian Belfast.

Richard Dawson Bates, the new Minister of Home Affairs, was a less judicious choice. The other members of the cabinet were responsible people and, according to their lights, kindly. They regarded Catholics as misguided but understood that some accommodation would have to be made with them some time in the future. Bates, 'a small man physically and intellectually', as Patrick Buckland described him in his short life of Craig, knew them to be traitors to king and the Empire. As far as he was concerned there were two types of Catholics: active members of the IRA and fellow travellers. His ministry, which had responsibility for the sensitive areas of local government, electoral affairs, and law and order, had great need of tact, flair and charisma, but it had none. His permanent staff members were as anti-nationalist as he, believing that the special crimes legislation should not be used against 'those who are loyal to the Crown'.

Bates's Civil Authorities (Special Powers) Bill became law on 7 April 1922, two days after the main police force became the Royal Ulster Constabulary (RUC). One MP, George Hanna, said with fine irony that the bill was too complicated: 'One section would have been sufficient: "The Home Secretary shall have the power to do what he likes or let somebody else do whatever he likes for him."' Craig had intended that membership of the RUC should be one third Catholic, roughly reflecting the population division. This proportion was never achieved and, by 1936, Catholics formed 17 percent of the total and a mere 11 percent in 1963. At the time of the change of name only 400 RIC Catholics transferred to the new 3,000-strong force. For some years there was a fair representation of Catholics among senior officers but from the start they experienced a sectarian prejudice that had not been a characteristic of the RIC. Soon it was realised that career prospects for Catholics were not great. This contrasted greatly with the treatment of members of the USC, who were given favourable entry conditions. The RUC were granted wide powers of arrest and detention, including internment without trial, and for years they faced one way. The Special Powers Act, as it was usually known, was kept on the statute book long after the threat of civil war was past and was made permanent in 1933. It was regarded with envy by the apartheid leaders in South Africa. Flogging of internees was common and the use of poison gas was not unknown. Churchill objected to the flogging but was told by Bates that it was legal under the terms of the act.

Joe Devlin did what he could to inform the largely uninterested British House of Commons about the true nature of law-keeping in Northern Ireland. On the day after the McMahon murders (that were followed by no investigation), he said: 'If Catholics have no revolvers to protect themselves they are murdered. If they have revolvers they are flogged and sentenced to death.'

Craig, who was already showing signs of the exhaustion and idleness that was to characterise his later premiership, probably deplored Bates's ultra-extremism but with a mixture of unease and inertia did nothing to curb it. The most dramatic use of the special powers occurred with the incarceration of 300 IRA suspects on the prison ship *Argenta* in 1922. On 20 May W J Twaddell, MP for West Belfast, was shot in the city centre on his way to his outfitters' shop. This was used over the next few weeks to 'lift' those believed to be active. The *Argenta* was a wooden ship of American manufacture originally berthed in Belfast Lough but moved round to Larne Lough for its penological purpose. The town had impeccable loyalist credentials and the narrowness of the lough made guarding it easier.

The internees were kept in cages forty feet by twenty feet by only eight feet high, which at times housed more than fifty inmates. There was extra 'accommodation' in the old Larne workhouse, where conditions were slightly better. Tuberculosis, pneumonia and other infectious diseases were rife in the appalling situation, and malnutrition was widespread because of rotten food. The internees were mainly middle class professionals who kept up their spirits by publishing the *Argenta Bulletin*, a samizdat, handwritten production wryly describing their imprisonment.

One of the contributors was a Westminster MP, Cahir Healy (1877–1970), who was elected Sinn Féin candidate for the Tyrone–Fermanagh constituency in 1922. A series of articles he wrote for the *Sunday Express* about prison conditions there and in Larne contributed to the internees' eventual release. Set free after his case was considered in the House of Commons, a debate involving bitter exchanges between the Conservatives and their opponents, he was rearrested when he broke an exclusion order preventing him from going to his home. He held the South Fermanagh seat at Stormont for forty years. His internment during World War II for two years caused another storm of protest.

The *Argenta* was regarded as a cheaper and more secure holding centre than any of the land centres. It was not until 1926 that all the internees were released and the hulk scuttled. It is indicative of the climate of the time and the mentality of the man that one of Bates's most prized souvenirs was the ship's bell.

Northern Catholics were shocked into total disarray and behaved as if they were living through a nightmare, which in a sense they were. In an oblique way they were victims not only of Protestant murder gangs but also of IRA activity. The only hope for people on the west bank of the Foyle in Derry, in Newry, and in the border areas of Tyrone, Fermanagh, Down, and Armagh was Article 12 of the Treaty which provided for a Boundary Commission to revise Northern Ireland's borders with the Free State. Their hopes were muted, however, because they could sense that the government, with its motley cabinet, seemed in spite of unconvincing huffing and puffing to be unconcerned about the commission's findings. There was an anticipatory sense of further betrayal that added to the general sense of 'this cannot be happening'.

On 22 August 1922 the Catholics of the north were dealt their severest blow: Michael Collins was killed in an ambush in his home county by 'irregulars', as the anti-Treaty forces were called. They felt that they had lost their only protection since Collins had, of all the members of the provisional government in the south, not been deflected from concern about Northern Ireland, and only he could have made the promised Boundary Commission have any value.

The commission met in London on 6 November 1924 for the first time. Northern Ireland was represented by the editor of the

Unionist *Northern Whig*, J R Fischer (1855–1939), appointed by London since Craig's government refused all cooperation, and Saorstát Éireann by Eóin MacNeill (1867–1945), the founder of the Irish Volunteers and Minister of Education. The chairman was Richard Feetham (1874–1965), a judge of the South African Supreme Court. Feetham was acceptable to Craig and therefore hardly neutral. Craig had threatened in October to resign with a characteristic speech promising to 'place myself, at the disposal of the people, no longer as Prime Minister but as their chosen leader, to defend any territory which we may consider has been unfairly transferred from under Ulster, Great Britain and the flag of our Empire'. It was at this time that the phrase 'not an inch', which he carried as a badge of pride, was first associated with him.

Ramsay MacDonald (1866–1937), briefly Prime Minister, was no more willing to risk 'more trouble in Ireland' than Lloyd George had been earlier. Feetham believed that it was not the work of the commission to redraw the border but to interpret Article 12. Its wording, 'to determine in accordance with the wishes of the inhabitants, so far as may be compatible with economic and geographic conditions, the boundaries between Northern Ireland and the rest of Ireland', was susceptible to many interpretations. The members toured the border areas throughout the next eleven months and Feetham finally decided that there would be virtually no change in the structure of Northern Ireland for 'economic and geographic reasons'. It suggested that more than 180,000 acres and 30,000 people in south Armagh be transferred to the Free State and something less than 50,000 acres and 7,600 people go from east Donegal to Northern Ireland. These findings were leaked to the ultra-Conservative *Morning Post* who published them on 7 October 1925 with a map showing the changes. MacNeill resigned in protest and the report was not published until 1969.

The northern Catholics felt utterly abandoned, especially when, on 3 December, a tripartite agreement between Craig, William

Cosgrave (1880–1965), the head of the Free State government, and Stanley Baldwin (1867–1947), the new Conservative premier, was signed revoking Article 12. The existing borders would remain, the Free State released from its Treaty obligation to the British national debt, and the two Irish governments agreeing to meet 'as and when necessary, for the purposes of considering matters of common interest'. There were to be few such meetings. Craig returned to Belfast 'happy and contented', a feeling not shared by border nationalists. The Catholics of Belfast and the four eastern counties, however, may have felt some comfort and confraternity in their mutual strength in the long, long struggle that lay ahead.

3

The New Regime

THE 'BORDER AGREEMENT', AS IT BECAME known, meant that the 70,000 Unionists of Donegal, Monaghan, and Cavan were placed in what their brethren in Northern Ireland would continue, right to the end of the century, to call the 'State'. They were not regarded with the same fear and distrust by Catholics there as the 340,000 Catholics were by northern Protestants. The Belfast *Irish News,* the main nationalist daily, on the day after the agreement, advised a kind of acquiescence:

> We are glad this Settlement has been made and signed… We have gained one advantage – and it is neither small nor mean: we have passed out of a period of uncertainty, deceit, false pretence and humbug, and we find ourselves face to face at last with stern realities of the situation which so many of us declined to consider during the past three or four years… The Nationalists of the Six Counties must look ahead, examine their political resources and resolve to utilise them, resist the tendency to indulge in recriminations… and realise once and for all that their fate in Ulster rests with themselves.

It was remarkably sensible advice and was taken by most nationalists to heart. Sick of the 'suffering and misery, unrest and ill-feeling', they were going to give the 'statelet' a chance. Their implicit acceptance was immediately spurned by Unionists and discouraged on the advice of the Catholic Church militant.

If the Unionist leadership had had any vestige of statesmanlike qualities the history of Northern Ireland might arguably have been very different. If Carson, the adamantine southern Unionist, had not left in a huff or if Craig (1st Viscount Craigavon of Stormont from 1927) had seen the need to consider the future, if he had had better health, or the courage to face down the Orange Order, his beloved Stormont might have lasted more than fifty years. As it was, he said in a speech at Stormont on 24 April 1934, 'I have always said that I am an Orangeman first and a politician and member of this parliament afterwards.' He goes down in history as the man who succeeded in obtaining Home Rule for Protestants and whose political career laid the seeds of its downfall.

Yet instead of reconciliation his actions – or inactions – gave Catholics no option but refusal to cooperate with his regime. The fact that he would have liked to have one third of the RUC Catholic and, after the pact with Collins, would have allowed Catholics into the USC, showed that he had an inkling of what was needed for political stability, but for the reasons mentioned above those ideals were not realised. Appointments to the civil service were similarly limited; between 1927 and 1959 the number of Catholics in the service was 6 percent with only one reaching the level of permanent secretary until Terence O'Neill (1914–1990) succeeded Lord Brookeborough (1883–1973) in 1963 as Prime Minister. This was Andrew Nicholas Bonaparte Wyse (1870–1940), who opted to serve in the North after partition but travelled home to Dublin each weekend. Pragmatic Catholics who were drawn to the civil service as a career wisely joined the Imperial civil service and were encouraged to do so by careers advisers in the schools. It meant for many perhaps a welcome exile but officers of HM Customs often applied successfully for home postings.

Catholics were being taught their place, a lesser breed barely tolerated by their masters. When on 12 July 1933 Sir Basil Brooke, afterwards Prime Minister (1943–63), speaking at the 'Twelfth' field in Newtownbutler in County Fermanagh, denounced those who employed Catholics, no one, least of all Catholics, was surprised. As the *Fermanagh Times* reported the occasion:

> There were a great number of Protestants and Orangemen who employed Roman Catholics. He felt he could speak freely on this subject as he had not a Roman Catholic about his own place… Roman Catholics were endeavouring to get in everywhere and were out with all their force and might to destroy the power and constitution of Ulster… He would appeal to Loyalists, therefore, wherever possible to employ good Protestant lads and lasses.

In fact Roman Catholics were not getting in anywhere and so it would continue in the large number of Unionist council areas, in the Fire Service, in hospitals (from consultants to ambulance drivers), and in the BBC. They greeted Brooke's appointment as Prime Minister ten years later with somewhat muted jubilation. He was characteristically unrepentant about his wounding and possibly inflammatory remarks. At a meeting of Londonderry Unionist Association on 20 March 1934 he repeated his remarks: 'I recommend those people who are Loyalists not to employ Roman Catholics, 99% of whom are disloyal… I want you to realise that, having done your bit, you have got your Prime Minister behind you.' He was speaking the simple truth, for next day at Stormont, Craigavon said, 'There is not one of my colleagues who does not agree with him, and I would not ask him to withdraw one word he said.'

The new government wasted little time in making its presence felt. As things grew quieter in the north the Unionist authorities, with characteristic ruthless efficiency, set about securing their permanent hegemony. As we have seen PR for local elections was soon abolished and ward boundaries were redrawn so as to maintain Protestant majorities. Derry was a notorious example of ward-rigging.

The term 'gerrymandering' had been imported from nineteenth-century Massachusetts, where the governor Elbridge Gerry had so rigged the boundaries in Essex County that the satirical artist Gilbert Stuart was able to outline them to look like a salamander. Benjamin Russell, the editor of the *Boston Sentinel*, remarked, 'Better call it a "gerrymander"' and the name stuck.

In Derry, Catholics with a majority of 5,000 had never been able to take control of the corporation because most of this majority was kept by means, usually foul, in the overcrowded South Ward and consequently was never able with their eight seats to outvote the eight North Ward Unionist councillors added to the four from the Waterside Ward. The boundaries were revised again in 1936. The lengths to which local Apprentice Boy lodges went to prevent Catholics buying property in the Unionist wards seem with hindsight unimaginable. If a potential Catholic buyer had made the highest offer for a house in the North Ward, the Waterside vendors were pressurised into accepting a lower offer from 'one of our own'. If this 'persuasion' failed, the difference might be made up out of 'funds'.

Derry was only one example of 'electoral redistribution'. Because of the abolition of PR, Unionists also gained control of the rural councils of Cookstown, Lisnaskea, Omagh, Dungannon, Magherafelt and Strabane; the county councils of Fermanagh and Tyrone; and the urban councils of Omagh (from 1935), Enniskillen and Armagh (from 1946). One cannot but admire the efficiency and single-mindedness that secured this deprivation of civil rights from the benighted one third of the population. They retained control of the urban and rural councils of Ballycastle and Newry; the urban district councils of Keady, Strabane, Downpatrick and Warrenpoint; and the rural council of Kilkeel.

Unionists, in defence of their policy of not promoting Catholics, used to point to equivalent practices in these Nationalist areas. However, as the Scarman Tribunal's report made clear, it was illogical to compare partial local job allocation in Newry, where there were very few Protestants, to areas like Derry, where there was a substantial Catholic majority. Catholics viewing the situation as a whole might well have quoted Shylock's muttered threat in *The Merchant of Venice*: 'The villainy you teach me I will execute, and it shall go hard but I will better the instruction.'

Later apologists claim that Catholics had only themselves to blame for their unfair treatment at the hands of their unassailable Unionist masters. It is true that they refused to take any part in the Leech committee that considered electoral boundaries and the Lynn committee that made recommendations about the future structure of education. Things, it was felt, had not yet been settled and cooperation might have obtained a better deal. The Catholic answer might well have been: why allow themselves to suffer rebuff and frustration. They had long experience of Unionist hostility and susceptibility to the influence of the Orange Order that had been founded in 1795 as a specifically anti-Catholic society. Each Prime Minister of Northern Ireland has been a member, and between 1921 and 1963, only three cabinet members were not Orangemen when they were elected. Catholics believed with some wisdom that application for membership of the committee chaired by John Leech (1857–1942), the Deputy Recorder of Belfast, was a waste of time. Even should they be given a place they would have been outvoted every time. In 1921, too, it was possible to believe that this essentially alien regime might not last. The Boundary Commission might find in favour of the nationalist regions of Tyrone, Fermanagh, Derry City, and South Armagh. In the meantime the statelet and its skewed organisations had to be protected, and chief among the councils that were to be made permanently safe for Unionism was the iconic city of Londonderry, as they persistently called it in public.

The education committee boycott had the same logical basis with the extra dimension of Church pressure. Sir Robert Lynn (1873–1945) was known, as a strong Orangeman, to be hostile to Catholics, and the absence of Catholics did not concern him greatly. The Church, notably those bishops whose dioceses were severed by the border – those of Clogher, Armagh and Derry – could not relinquish their canonical control. They were bound in conscience to make sure that the classroom, the second most potent source of the development of the Catholic ethos, should be directed as far as possible according to Church teaching. The Lynn committee's findings formed the basis for Lord Londonderry's 1923 Education Act that essentially proposed secular education for primary schools (or public elementary schools, as they were then called). There were to be three types of schools: those wholly maintained by local authorities, voluntary schools under 'four and two' committees, and other voluntary schools. The 'four' were assumed to be representatives of the church 'owners' and the 'two' local authority representatives. The first category of school should essentially be maintained by central and local government funding; the second type received half the expenses of heating, cleaning and maintenance from discretionary capital local authority grants; while the third group were given no money for capital expenditure, though in practice half of their heating, lighting and cleaning costs were paid from the local rates. Teachers' salaries would be paid in all three types of school by central government.

Secular education proved not to be acceptable to many Protestants as well. In December 1924 Anglican, Presbyterian and Methodist school managers formed the United Education Committee (UEC) and, joining forces with the Orange Order, began a campaign using the cry 'Protestants awake' to have the terms of the act changed. They warned that the act permitted bolshevists, atheists or Roman Catholics to teach in Protestant schools. Schools were made safe for Protestant children, and Catholics bore the brunt and the cost of their independence. Eventually Catholics accepted the 'four and two' system when they felt, or rather their pastors felt, there were sufficient safeguards. Neil Farren, Bishop of Derry (1939–74), indicated in 1945 the Church's main concern was that the 'four' had, according to the government, to be laypersons. He said that that requirement was spurious, 'since the clergy were always accepted by the Catholic people as their natural representatives'.

It is difficult as Irish society grows more secular to realise how much Catholics were influenced by, and perhaps depended upon, the hierarchy. These battles seem ancient now since educational grants are generous and virtually non-denominational. Yet the Church's attitude then was summarised by northern bishops in their statement in 1921: Catholic children were to be educated in Catholic schools with a Catholic ethos; teachers were to be trained in Catholic teacher training colleges and appointed by Catholic clerical managers, who would also supervise their textbooks.

The admonition about training colleges meant that since St Patrick's, Drumcondra in Dublin, the chief men's education college in Ireland, was no longer available, alternative arrangements had to be made. For a number of years in the early 1920s Catholic students attended the secular college at Stranmillis in Belfast with religious education at St Mary's College, the women's college, in the Falls Road. Eventually accommodation was found for them in St Mary's at Strawberry Hill, the 'little Gothic castle' built by the writer Horace Walpole (1717–97). For a few years after World War II men were again accommodated in the women's training college until a male college, eventually called St Joseph's, was prepared on the Andersontown Road.

As far as Catholic secondary schools were concerned canon law, originating in the counter-reformation Council of Trent (1545–63), was specific. It required of bishops that they establish junior diocesan seminaries for the early education of students for the priesthood. The purpose they later served as providing education for a Catholic laity was almost an afterthought. Education for girls was provided almost exclusively by teaching orders of nuns with, of course, lay assistance. No one expected this system to change.

Catholics accepted the financial stringency as the price of spiritual independence and Northern Ireland accepted denominational education. The exception was that offered by technical colleges where those preparing with practical subjects to be plumbers, builders and electricians were taught, and where Catholics and Protestants mingled with no visible personal disadvantage. Those who graduated from these non-denominational institutes avoided the trap of revealing their 'colour' since, though it was illegal for application forms to ask for the candidate's religion, the place of education generally gave the information.

The two-tribe system covert in the nineteenth century was now overt. The masters were Protestant and much more likely to be in employment, while the Catholics, often showing 'victim' psychology, maintained a separate culture. In practice there was little territorial segregation. In most towns members of the tribes were next door neighbours. For historical reasons the poorer areas tended to be Catholic though there were poor Protestants as well. Middle class areas were what in the Gaeltacht – with, of course, a linguistic and not a political sense – would be called *breac* ('speckled'). Catholics and Protestants lived in formal amity. There was no colour bar nor were physical tribal characteristics all that reliable, in spite of boasts by both sides. Orange, crimson and black marches were seasonal events and where it was safe there were also green ones, notably on St Patrick's Day and on 15 August, the feast of the Assumption. Outside of Belfast there was general support of local soccer teams, golf clubs had mixed membership, and the dole queues were non-sectarian.

Protestants were forced to maintain the wearisome siege mentality, with exaltation tending to leech away in the light of common day. Catholic non-cooperation caused in them the same kind of paranoia but they felt a genuine kinship with their brethren in the Free State, even if it was not always reciprocated in practice. Their sense of being participant in a wider, older culture gave a positive cohesion.

They were cheered by the regular irredentist noises from Dublin and tended to read, as well as local nationalist papers, the Dublin dailies, the *Irish Independent* and, after 1931, even more enthusiastically, the *Irish Press*. Cultivation of the *Irish Times* was a much later phenomenon, produced by that paper's greening.

A majority of nationalists, with the cheerful pragmatism that had enabled them to survive since penal times, acquiesced in the often penal conditions of life in what they dismissively called the Six Counties. They regarded themselves as the co-inheritors of both the Gaelic tradition and the fruits of the Irish cultural renaissance. The Gaelic Athletic Association (GAA), sometimes called 'common low-class Gaels' (a pun on the Irish name of the association: Cumann Luthchleas Gael), was a uniting force, though slightly less so in soccer towns like Derry, Coleraine, Lurgan and Newry. The Irish language, part of the curriculum of all secondary schools since the 1890s, the féiseanna (music, language and dance festivals) held annually in most nationalist areas, and Radió Éireann that began broadcasting as 2RN on 1 January 1926 – all kept the tradition alive. In 1924, from the 2nd to the 17th of August, the Tailteann Games in Croke Park marked the Free State's first assertion of its individuality. The title came from the prehistoric Aonach Tailteann, a kind of Celtic Olympic Games. The modern event included shooting, cycling and motorcycle races, and was repeated in 1928 and 1932. It was celebrated throughout Ireland with expected exceptions.

BBC Northern Ireland began on 15 September 1924 as '2BE, the Belfast Station of the British Broadcasting Corporation', as its first announcer, the young Tyrone Guthrie (1900–71), described it. It did not live up to the BBC watch cry of 'Nation shall speak unto nation.' In 1937 the BBC Northern Region intended to produce in Manchester a programme with the title, *The Irish*. George L Marshall, the Belfast station's second director, objected:

> My first reaction would have been that the very title itself was highly

undesirable, linking under one name two strongly antipathetic states with completely different political outlooks. There is no such thing today as an Irishman. One is either a citizen of the Irish Free State or a citizen of the United Kingdom of Great Britain and Northern Ireland. Irishmen as such ceased to exist after partition.

The nice sending of now nearly half a million nationalists who lived in Northern Ireland but did not hold allegiance to the UK into limbo sums up the region's attitude. Succeeding controllers saw it as their duty to do nothing that would rattle the government's position. At times it seemed that Glengall Street and not Ormeau Avenue was BBC NI's headquarters.[1] Writing in the autobiographical *The Middle of My Journey* (1990) about his own experience as a professional broadcaster, John Boyd (1912–2001) described the station to which he was appointed in 1946 as Talks Producer:

The staff in Broadcasting House contained only a few Catholics, of whom none held senior posts, and none were producers. This was no accident but a deliberate policy of exclusion. Catholics were considered untrustworthy of posts of responsibility, and many years had to pass before the question of religious discrimination was confronted.

By the end of the 1920s Northern Ireland had taken on the rigid structures that were to characterise it for nearly forty further years. Catholics made the best life they could in spite of all their political disabilities. They developed a fine perception of economic realities and learned to survive. Northern Ireland's own economy was sluggish and unemployment was high, unsurprisingly highest in such 'unreliable' towns as Derry and Strabane.

Derry suffered greatly because of partition. It went from being one of the most prosperous and go-ahead places in Ireland to becoming an economic black spot with an unemployment level of 26 percent. The loss of its hinterland of Donegal and Sligo had dire consequences for the city as a whole and for the possibilities of male employment. Its young men had, like so many of their brothers in the south, to take to the 'emigrant's boat' and cause the final departure of more than 3,000 citizens. Derry's shirt factories, with its female workforce, gave the city what little buoyancy it retained and had an interesting effect on the nature of the city's social life. Yet, even here, the managerial staff was largely Protestant. Catholics developed perforce a grim sense of humorous acceptance. They were amused rather than shocked that, when Dawson Bates heard 'with a great deal of surprise' that a Catholic telephonist had been appointed in Stormont, he refused to use the phone until the telephonist was dismissed.

The ending of PR for parliamentary elections in 1927 was greeted with the same forbearance as the appearance of British and Free State customs posts on the border that lay only three miles from Derry, across the river from Strabane, and ran down through the town of Pettigo in Fermanagh/Donegal, causing one half of the town during World War II to be blacked-out according to Ministry of Defence regulations while the other half in neutral Éire (from 1936) blazed with normal light.

4

The Hungry Thirties

The Wall Street Crash of October 1929 was followed by the world slump still known as the Great Depression. The already ailing economy of Northern Ireland was badly affected. Shipbuilding and the linen industry declined, the latter missing badly the strong demand from the US. In shipbuilding Workman Clark, the smaller of the two 'yards' and source of the 1920 industrial evictions, closed in 1935, and linen became a luxury item. Unemployment in the 1930s rose to 27 percent and many workers were forced on to outdoor relief. Welfare limped behind Britain and did not catch up until after World War II. Labour movements did badly because among Protestants membership of the Orange Order, though it paid no direct financial benefits, was regarded by working class people as having sufficient cachet to compensate for, at times, cynical manipulation. Jim Larkin (1876–1947), the great trade union organiser, had managed to unite Protestant and Catholic workers briefly during the Belfast dock strike of 1907 but found himself frustrated by the employers' playing of the Orange Card and dividing the dockers' solidarity by resurrecting the old sectarian fears. One of his speeches on the subject was replicated by Michael McLaverty (1904–92) in his novel *Call My Brother Back* (1939):

Supposin' ye got all the Orange sashes and all the Green sashes in this town and ye tied them round loaves of bread and flung them over the Queen's Bridge, what would happen?… The gulls – the gulls that fly in the air, what would they do? They'd go for the bread! But *you* – the other Gulls – would go for the sashes every time!

There came a time in 1932 during a period of high unemployment when cuts in outdoor relief and family means testing, and its parsimonious administration by Poor Law Guardians, led to united public disorder with both sides briefly joining forces to demonstrate against the system. Belfast's relief dole was the lowest in the United Kingdom at 60p (twelve shillings) a week for a married couple with one child, compared with Liverpool's rate of £1.15 and Bradford's £1.30. Unmarried people got no payment at all. Half of the statelet's unemployment afflicted Belfast, and it was notorious both for its infant mortality and the malnutrition of the survivors. The city had, in spite of its endemic sectarianism, some labour agitation. It should be remembered that a quarter of those driven out of employment in the early 1920s were not Catholics but Protestant socialists, feared perhaps even more by the Unionist establishment than Catholics/ nationalists. Craig's abolition of PR in parliamentary elections was directed as much against organised labour as against the more obvious adversary. Communists, especially the Revolutionary Workers Groups (RWG), were detested, particularly as the chief organisers of the outdoor relief strike of October 1932.

It began on the first Monday of that month and lasted for about ten days. There were protest marches, torch-lit processions and rioting in both Catholic and Protestant areas when, on 11 October, the RUC tried to ban a march. The main concentration of police was as usual in the lower Falls where they used rifles and revolvers, killing a Protestant flower seller called Samuel Baxter and John Keegan, a Catholic from Smithfield. The following evening there was trouble in York Street when the RUC fired on looters, killing John Kennan from Leeson Street and wounding many others. The government, already rattled by protests by Protestant clergy and businessmen, capitulated on 14 October, forcing the guardians to provide more money. They gave £1 for a married couple, £1.20 for a couple with one or two children, and so on, in a sliding scale to a maximum of £1.60 for a couple with five or more children.

It was a mighty victory but in the bitter Belfast of the 1930s the workers' solidarity was to be soon dissipated. Faced with the prospect of a united workforce certain members of the establishment encouraged a resurgence of overt Protestant dominance. The effective persuasion was the old cry of danger to the state by 'disloyalists', a description that was simplistically applied to all non-Unionists. The siege mentality persisted, strengthened by the success of de Valera in the 1932 election and the setting-up of a Fianna Fáil government. 'Partition must go' became a recurrent war-cry at hustings in the Free State but no action was intended or implemented. It remained as a mere mantra. De Valera's growing reputation as a statesman of international status, especially his appointment as chairman of the League of Nations in 1932, rankled, as did the enthusiasm generated by the 31st Eucharistic Congress when thousands of northern Catholics travelled to Dublin to swell the numbers who attended the Mass in the Phoenix Park to a million. The trains and buses that brought back the pilgrims were attacked at Banbridge, Lurgan, Portadown and Lisburn, among other places. Most Catholic houses were decorated with a specially designed blue Congress cross. There was, undoubtedly, a certain, perhaps forgivable, triumphalism about the Irish Church at the time but it gave Catholics, especially the Catholics of Northern Ireland, a sense of a wider belonging, a reminder that the word with a small 'c' meant universal. Unsophisticated Protestants found themselves afflicted again with atavistic fears and it was comparatively easy to revive militancy.

An extremist group called the Ulster Protestant League (UPL), founded in 1931, grew steadily in numbers as the decade advanced, supported publicly by members of the Unionist parliamentary party.

The generation of such a group as the UPL had occurred before and would again. Whenever there seemed to be the possibility of a kind of peace and a diminution of sectarianism there were always to be found diehards who would attack any hope of reconciliation. The UPL forgave those Protestants who had been misled by communists during the 1932 strike. The annual trumpeting at Twelfth 'fields' did nothing to calm fears or suggest an end to tribal suspicion. As there was widespread unemployment that affected even loyal, hardworking, frugal Protestants the prospect of Catholics having jobs and beginning to evolve a middle class was for some extremist hotheads too much to bear. In November 1933 a Catholic publican called Dan O'Boyle was shot dead in York Street. There was intermittent violence against Catholics in 1934. In September forty Catholic homes were destroyed in the now vanished Marine Street and New Dock Street, resulting in the death of a cripple who was unable to move to a place of safety and was killed when a kerbstone was thrown through his window. Nineteen thirty-five, the silver jubilee of the accession of George V, gave Belfast Protestants the equivalent euphoria that the Eucharistic Congress had given to Catholics two years earlier. A Catholic was shot dead in his shop in Great George's Street, off York Street, and in May and June twenty-six people were injured.

On 18 June Dawson Bates, still Minister of Home Affairs, banned all parades and Sir Joseph Davison, Grand Master of the Orange Order, responded with 'You may be perfectly certain that on the Twelfth of July Orangemen will be marching throughout Northern Ireland.' And, of course, they did. Craigavon was off on one of the many cruises that characterised the last decade of his life and Bates, conscious of the role that the Order played in the fabric of the state, rescinded his ban.

The speeches at the various venues on the Twelfth were as inflammatory as ever and trouble broke out when 40,000 marchers swaggered down Royal Avenue on their way back to their dispersal point. It took very little to start the affray but the riots continued sporadically for three weeks. On the evening of the Twelfth a breakaway group of mainly Glaswegians smashed windows in Lancaster Street until they were driven back down to York Street again by resisting Catholics. Until the end of August there was nightly rioting with mobile barbed-wire entanglements put in place by military and police to separate the mobs. In all, eight Protestants and eight Catholics died with many wounded, mainly Catholic. Two-and-a-half thousand Catholics were driven from their homes in York Street, Old Lodge Road and Donegall Road, taking refuge in the Falls Road and Ardoyne. Ninety-five percent of the £22,000 paid in compensation was given to Catholics. Daniel Mageean, the Bishop of Down and Connor, managed to have the matter raised in the House of Commons but Stanley Baldwin, the Prime Minister, with typical Conservative dismissal, said the matter 'was entirely within the discretion and responsibility of the government of Northern Ireland'.

The Westminster attitude had, since 1920, been, and would continue to be until the end of the 1960s, rather like that of the headmaster and staff of an English public school. They left matters of discipline to the senior prefects who would have the power to keep the junior common room under control. They would have liked the regime to replicate the British system with civil liberties and equality of opportunity irrespective of race or creed but they would take the prefects' word that the juniors were not quite ready for such privileges. The metaphorical headmaster and his staff stayed aloof except for stately appearances at school concerts and prize days. It was only when the state collapsed in the early 1970s because of its moral and structural flaws that Westminster was forced to dismiss these dysfunctional prefects and face the roaring boys in person.

Catholics, their instinctive amenability despised, could when roused be as dangerous as their adversaries and some parades of the Ancient Order of Hibernians (AOH) appeared as triumphalist as any Twelfth walk. The Order had been founded in America in 1836 to succour Irish immigrants and maintain confraternity within the Irish-American community. It was imported in 1900 and gathered members in Britain as well as Ireland. 'Wee Joe' Devlin made it into a highly successful political machine but its essential constitutionalism held no appeal for the more radical Sinn Féin; after 1921 it seemed merely a weaker green version of the Orange Order, earning its members the jibing nickname, mainly among Catholics, of the Ancient Order of Catholic Orangemen. The banners, sashes and marches, though brilliantly green and resplendent with gold harps, seemed theatrical and unconvincing, a kind of throwback to the even more gorgeously uniformed but entirely apolitical Irish National Foresters. The AOH now mainly exists in a severely contracted form as a charitable organisation.

'Wee Joe' Devlin's death on 18 February 1934 was a serious blow to nationalist Belfast, especially the poor of the Falls Road area, whose champion he never ceased to be. Unmarried, he regularly financed excursions for poor children and established from his own finances a holiday home for their sorely tried mothers. Though bitterly critical of Unionist rule he had friends in the party, once taking Craigavon to greyhound racing in Celtic Park in the nationalist end of the Donegall Road. He felt bitterly betrayed by what he perceived as the Free State's dereliction of responsibility for northern Catholics. His funeral was huge and, even though he regularly excoriated them with his prodigious oratorical powers, Unionist government officials joined representatives from all other political parties to follow his coffin.

The privation of the early 1930s that Devlin fought so valiantly continued right to the end of Auden's 'low dishonest decade'. Poverty was endemic with many people at the level of subsistence in appalling slums. Apart from agriculture, which had retained some buoyancy, most of Northern Ireland's industries reflected its stasis in politics. 'Cap-in-hand' is perhaps a crude description of the approach of finance ministers to the Westminster treasury but Northern Ireland's position was little short of dependency. The members of the cabinet were not especially gifted, appointed as safe pairs of hands rather than possessing specific political talent.

They met in the splendid new parliament buildings at Stormont that had been a gift of the British government and was royally opened by David, Prince of Wales (1894–1972) – later Edward VIII and, later still, Duke of Windsor – on 16 November 1932. Facing southwest and set in 300 acres of beautiful parkland, three and a half miles from the city centre, its white neo-classical opulence, designed by Sir Arnold Thornby of Liverpool, was in stark contrast to the poverty of the city. On 30 September 1932, at the last session of parliament in the City Hall, where the members had met since 22 June 1921, Jack Beattie of the Northern Ireland Labour Party (NILP), MP for Pottinger, threw the mace, Cromwell-like, to the floor in a protest about the government's complacency about mass unemployment. Hugh McDowell Pollock, the Finance Minister, however, spoke with true Unionist fervour, seeing in the new buildings 'the outward and visible proof of the permanence of our institutions; that for all time we are bound indissolubly to the British crown'. It was a permanence that was to last forty years, and though never betraying it outwardly, a binding somewhat uncomfortable for the crown.

Craigavon, now essentially a part-time premier, gave little leadership, though he was capable of reaction if there seemed to be any threat to the partition, his own creation. Ramsay McDonald's son, Malcolm (1901–81), a liberal and clever Dominions Secretary, successfully negotiated the end of the Free State's (known officially as Éire since 29 December 1937) economic war with Britain in 1938. The announcement of the important meetings between the two countries' ministers raised nationalist hopes that perhaps the exasperating and, as they saw it, grossly immoral border might disappear. It raised a corresponding fear among Unionists that in their endlessly repeated watchword, 'what we have we hold', might be at risk. Bates neatly summed up their thinking in an address to the loyal women of the Victoria Ward that was reported in the *Irish News* on 30 March:

> So long as we live there will always be the danger of Home Rule or merging into the Free State... We have this continual menace at our doors – a menace that will last as long as we live.

As usual northern nationalists were disappointed; their situation was often referred to by de Valera but he was too astute a politician to assail such rooted entrenchment. Unification remained a pious hope, not even an ambition. He had plenty to concern himself with the problem of the annuities and the disposition of the naval ports retained by Britain under the terms of the Treaty. Cork harbour and Lough Swilly were recovered, much to the distress of Churchill, who was certain of a coming war with Germany. Speaking in the House of Commons on 5 May in fine rhetorical flow, he warned:

> These ports are in fact the sentinel towers of the western approaches, by which the forty-five million people in this island so enormously depend on foreign food for their daily bread... Now we are to give them up, unconditionally, to an Irish government led by men – I do not want to use harsh words – whose rise to power has been proportionate to the animosity to which they have acted against this country. The ports may be denied us in the hour of need... it will be no use saying, 'then we will retake the ports'... To violate Irish neutrality should it be declared at the moment of a great war may put you out of court in the opinion of the world.

The ports were to play their part in a slightly surreal incident when war actually came.

Meanwhile Northern Ireland subsisted on handouts, locked in adamantine determination to preserve its separate integrity and eternally fearful of its 'disloyal' and second-class minority. Even its most sanguine civil servants knew the situation was dire; 'it could not go on!' And then, as in 1914, they were saved by what was a cataclysm to most of the rest of the world. Just as the Kaiser's territorial ambitions prevented the UVF from having to live up to its threats of armed resistance to even limited Home Rule, so the aftermath of Munich and the invasion of Poland on 1 September 1939 deflected the attention of Britain from Northern Ireland's poor economic performance.

5

Not a Bad War

THE OUTBREAK OF WAR ON SUNDAY, 3 September 1939
was used by several interested parties in Ireland as an opportunity for
advantage. The IRA, the rump of hardliners who had not accepted
the Treaty or joined Fianna Fáil's now constitutional party, under
their leader, Sean Russell (1893–1940), acting as chief-of-staff of
what he insisted was the only true government of Ireland, had sent a
letter to Downing Street on 12 January 1939 demanding the
withdrawal of all British armed forces in Ireland, such intention to
be shown within four days: 'Our government reserves the right of
appropriate action without further notice if on the expiration of the
period of grace these conditions remain unfulfilled.' The letter that
the senders knew would be ignored was merely to give some legitimacy
to the bombing campaign that followed in Britain. The IRA declared
war on Britain after the four-day period and between then and July
there were 127 explosions, seven deaths and 200 serious injuries. As
with later campaigns the only real victims were the exiled Irish who
bore the brunt of complaint from their neighbours. Russell headed
for Germany to train as a spy but on his return journey to Ireland by
U-boat he died. His campaign gave retroactive approval to the
internment of forty-five Ulster members on 22 December 1938.[1]

The war affected 'both sides of the house', to use the persistent metaphor that still sums up the condition of Northern Ireland, but in rather different ways. There was a whiff of Churchill's 'dreary spires' in nationalists' wondering how the war would affect the question of partition. With little political acuity and on the principle that 'my enemy's enemy is my friend' some northern nationalists went to Dublin to a meeting with Dr Edouard Hempel, the German ambassador, and placed the Catholic minority under the protection of the Axis powers.

The IRA campaign sputtered out, largely because de Valera took and continued to take stringent action against them that neither Westminster nor Stormont would have dared, including internment and the refusal to release hunger strikers. They had some support in the north, being accused of blackout infringements in west Belfast that included shining torches from roofs to guide the Luftwaffe during air raids and ceremoniously burning respirators. These gasmasks were supplied to all citizens soon after the Sunday morning broadcast of Neville Chamberlain (1858–1941). Cinema newsreels of the time showed the people of the United Kingdom going cheerfully to work with their respirators slung round their shoulders but apart from service personnel, RUC officers and ARP (Air Raid Precautions) wardens, they were not carried in Northern Ireland. There were less frightening ones for younger children, coloured red and blue with a kind of beak, almost as though Walt Disney had been working for the War Office. In 1941 a further filter was added against mustard gas and people having their respirators adjusted were given a noxious whiff of the stuff as a sharp reminder of their purpose.

Leaflets about what to do in an air raid were sent to each house in Northern Ireland and they too ended up on bonfires in nationalist areas. Rationing of food began in 1940 with butter, bacon and sugar affected in January, meat in March. A 'points' system for tinned goods was introduced in June 1942 and similarly for clothes, when trousers turn-ups disappeared and less cloth was used for 'utility' suits. Sweets disappeared from the shops in the months before rationing began, to reappear magically when the ubiquitous ration books were delivered. This fustian booklet and the slimmer identity card went everywhere, even on holidays, since seaside landladies could not buy provisions without them.

Rationing persisted into the post-war 'austerity' period, sweets still requiring coupons until 1953. These measures were organised with tolerable bureaucratic efficiency as was the distribution of cod liver oil and concentrated orange juice that was part of the lease-lend arrangement agreed between Franklin Delano Roosevelt (1882–1945) and Churchill, Prime Minister from May 1940, before America entered the war.

The same efficiency did not characterise Stormont or its geriatric cabinet. They persisted in the belief that there would be no attack from the air because of the distance that bombers would have to fly from German soil. They continued with this 'ostrichism' even when the *Wehrmacht* were manning coastal batteries in Brittany and had occupied the Channel Islands.

One thing not in doubt was their loyalty to Britain and their willingness to die for the cause. At least that was the message that the ailing Craigavon kept sending to Chamberlain, almost to the point of embarrassment. What *did* cause embarrassment was Craigavon's insistence, almost plea, that conscription should be imposed on Northern Ireland as in the rest of the United Kingdom. This in fact would have meant the conscription of nationalists since a majority of Protestants were in reserved occupations. The threat of conscription galvanised the minority community in May 1939 and they were supported in this by the Church. Chamberlain was forced to ask Craigavon to desist, saying: 'If you really want to help us don't press for conscription. It will only be an embarrassment.'

The question of conscription arose again in May 1941, the nadir of the Allies' fortunes in the war. Cardinal MacRory (1861–1945), a veteran of the pogroms, since he was Bishop of Down and Connor in the early 1920s, argued that if imposed it 'would seek to compel those who writhe under this grievous wrong [partition by a foreign power] to fight on the side of the perpetrators'. A further anti-conscription campaign culminated in a mass rally in Belfast attended by 10,000 protesters. John Andrews, who had become Prime Minister on Craigavon's death on 24 November 1940, personally contacted the Home Office to advise against it. On 27 May 1941 Churchill, who had replaced Chamberlain, announced that conscription would not be imposed in Northern Ireland, saying that it would be more trouble than it was worth to enforce.

That, however, did not prevent volunteering. Recruitment fell from 2,500 a month in the early days of the war to 600 a year later. Among those 'called up' were members of the Territorial Army who, though weekend soldiers, were mobilised in the last days of August 1939. In Derry the 'terries' formed the 24th and 25th heavy anti-aircraft batteries who by Halloween in the first year of the war found themselves in Egypt. In all, about 38,000 people from Northern Ireland enlisted in the forces with an approximately equal number from Éire. Craigavon decided that the B-specials should form the basis of the Home Guard, leaving the growing nationalist majority excluded because of certainly exaggerated doubts about its loyalty.

On the Home Front, to use the patriotic term employed at the time, Northern Ireland did tolerably well. Agriculture, the only good performer in the 1930s, was to the fore with doubled acreage under tillage and an annual export of £3 million worth of livestock and 20 percent of Britain's eggs. Twenty-five thousand gallons of milk were sent each day to Scotland. The shipyards built six aircraft carriers, more than 130 other warships and 123 cargo ships, and carried out repairs to over 3,000 damaged vessels. The factories built tanks and produced millions of aircraft parts. Strikes were illegal in wartime but unofficial walkouts occurred frequently. It was generally believed that not all the operatives' working time was spent in the war effort.

One of the stories from the urban folklore of the time concerns the visit of a VIP to the Short and Harland aircraft factory, one of the few industries that was brought to Northern Ireland by the state incentives of the 1930s. The personage asked one worker how many fighters they made in a week. The worker answered, 'Twenty.' The VIP said, 'Twenty fighters! Why that's magnificent!' The worker sighed, 'Sorry. I thought you said lighters.'

As Churchill had foretold, the loss of the retained ports was a serious blow to the Allies as the U-boats seemed likely to win the Battle of the Atlantic and cut off Britain's desperately needed supplies of imported goods, including foodstuffs. Though not particularly fond of the man, because of the loss of the ports that he had negotiated, Churchill sent Malcolm MacDonald to try to persuade de Valera to come in on the side of the Allies on the promise of a united Ireland after the war. As MacDonald put it to de Valera on 26 June 1940: '…on the assumption that Éire had carried out its part of the plan, it was unthinkable that the promise would be broken'. Next day, Craigavon, having been told by letter by Churchill of the negotiations, sent an agonised telegram to him:

> Am profoundly shocked and disgusted by your letter making suggestions so far reaching behind my back and without any preconsultation with me. To such treachery to loyal Ulster I will never be a party.

The War Office, reeling at the German conquest of mainland Europe, would have promised anything but with the precedent of Britain's shabby treatment of John Redmond in the Great War, and determined on maintaining neutrality, de Valera rejected the rather vague offer. His view of the nature of the German threat was slightly different from Britain's. He probably expected, as did most of the rest of the world, that Hitler would be victorious, and was too tough-minded to see such a victory as the end of western civilisation. Throughout his career many commentators achieved nothing but frustration trying to read his mind. His great adversary,

David Gray, the US ambassador in Dublin, summed him up well in a dispatch to Roosevelt on 10 November 1940: 'No one can outwit him, frighten him or brandish him. Remember he is not pro-German nor personally anti-British but only pro-de Valera.' His refusal made him very unpopular except, of course, at home and among nationalists in the north. Even so vigorous a supporter of Ireland as the poet Louis MacNeice, the Home Ruler son of a Home Ruler father, wrote a bitter condemnatory poem called 'Neutrality', ending with the lines: 'While to the west off your own shores the mackerel/Are fat with the flesh of your kin.'

Churchill made another attempt to recover the ports in his telegram of 8 December 1941 with the message: 'Now is your chance. Now or never. "A nation once again." Am very ready to meet you at any time.' De Valera replied six days later: 'We can only be a friendly neutral.' Churchill's words were somewhat Delphic; it was not quite clear what he was offering. It may have been no more than an admonition that Éire should shape up.

The ports became less significant with the entry of America into the war after 7 December 1941 when the Japanese bombed Pearl Harbor. The port of Derry became central to the war effort, serving less adequately the same purpose that neighbouring Lough Swilly had in the Great War. On 30 June 1941, six months before Pearl Harbor, nearly 400 American 'technicians' arrived to prepare for the US forces that were certainly going to come and whose presence on Irish soil would be predictably objected to by de Valera as 'occupation'. They built a submarine school in the grounds of an unused distillery, a graving dock to facilitate repairs to damaged shipping, accommodation camps and new quays.

Derry was shaken both psychologically and economically out of its Thirties torpor. Men who had been on the dole for years found employment and the Yanks, as they were congenially, if inaccurately, called, were less aware of nationalist 'unsuitability' for work as former employers. There were sweets for the children, different chewing gum, Hershey bars and Baby Ruth chocolate. Their fathers began to smoke Camel, Philip Morris and Lucky Strikes, of which there seemed to be no scarcity. Their sisters found lots of new, temporary boyfriends, and Neil Farren of Derry, still Ireland's youngest bishop, was appointed 'ordinary' to American forces in Ireland. By May 1942 there were 37,000 of these generous exotics and the terminally depressed town became for a few years a lesser Babylon on the Foyle, with doughboys, sailors (for a five-day turnaround in the only place where, they swore, they needed their heavy clothes) and marines. At times when the prevailing Atlantic airflow brought Derry's famous rains, old native-born Californians would cry: 'Why don't they pull out the plug and let the [expletive deleted] place sink!' Airfields were built on suitable tracts on flat land along the shores of Lough Foyle, at Eglinton and Ballykelly, at Toome and other places, bringing the headiness of these friendly aliens throughout the 'six occupied counties'. Just before D-Day there were 120,000 GIs in the north, for so many their last weeks on earth.

The war did not afflict Northern Ireland as fiercely as it did other parts of Britain. The number of service casualties was less than 5,000, 500 of these merchant seamen. A Catholic, James Megennis, won the Victoria Cross in a naval action near Singapore in 1945. In spite of the politicians' self-reassurance – a feeling shared by most of the population – that the north would never be a target for aerial bombardment, Belfast came face to face with the terrors of modern warfare on four spring nights in 1941.

Craigavon's successor, John Andrews, had no real grasp of what needed to be done to try to secure the safety of the citizens of a city that was an obvious target because of its shipyards, if nothing else. In November 1940 a German reconnaissance plane had brought back photographs of among others, *die Werft Harland & Wolff* (the Harland & Wolff shipyard), *das Fleugzeugwerk Short & Harland* (the Short and Harland aircraft works), *das Kraftwerk Belfast* (the Belfast power station), *die Grossmühle Rank* (the Rank mills), and *das Wasserwerk Belfast* (the Belfast waterworks). It also discovered that the city had only seven anti-aircraft batteries.

The raid on the night of 7–8 April 1941 that badly damaged part of Harland & Wolff and the docks, and killed thirteen people, was just a taster. Easter Tuesday, 15 April, brought 180 German bombers that devastated the civilian areas of the lower Shankill and Antrim Roads. The destruction of the main telephone exchange cut off communications with the anti-aircraft placements and with Britain. Though 200 tonnes of high explosive bombs and 800 incendiaries fell there was virtually no return of fire. Nearly 800 people died, and since the city mortuaries could not house them, the Falls Road swimming baths were drained and 150 bodies were laid out there. Two hundred and fifty were taken to St George's Market and the unclaimed bodies were buried in a mass grave on the following Monday. Bombs also fell on Newtownards and Bangor. De Valera was anxious to help and sent a total of thirteen appliances and seventy fire-fighters from Dundalk, Drogheda and Dublin; they found their way in the blackout by following the telegraph wires.

The west of the province had its visit from the Luftwaffe that night too. A single bomber dropped two mines in Derry to hit the graving dock but they missed their target. One fell on Messines Park, a street built for ex-servicemen from the Great War and called after the battle fought near Ypres on 7 June 1917. It demolished five houses and killed fifteen people. The other fell into a sandpit, slightly damaging St Patrick's Church. One watcher 'saw' the statue of the saint in the main tower push the mine away from the church. It now seems odd with the wisdom of hindsight that Derry was not seriously targeted. It was essentially the head of operations of western approaches and the station from which the U-boat menace was defeated and the Battle of the Atlantic was won.

The raids in May were characterised by firestorms caused by the 6,000 incendiaries that found appropriate targets in the shipyards and Shorts. Though the April raids had resulted in the deaths of more people in one raid in any city except London, the death toll for May was much smaller at less than 200. The damage to property was extensive and the flames were seen by Derry fire crews from the top of Glenshane Pass forty miles away. One of the reasons for the lower fatality figure was the exodus of refugees from the city. There were moments when sectarian differences were forgotten as women and children from the Shankill and the Falls sought sanctuary in the Redemptorist monastery at Clonard. Dawson Bates, predictable as ever, described 5,000 refugees as absolutely 'unbilletable owing to personal habits which are subhuman'. He did not seem to realise that their condition was an indictment of the government of which he was Minister of Home Affairs for twenty years of bad social practice.

A German radio reporter, Ernst von Kurhen, who flew with one of the squadrons, reported that 'in Belfast there was not just a large number of conflagrations but just one enormous conflagration that spread over the entire harbour and industrial area… Here the English… felt themselves safe, far up in the north, safe from the blows of the German airforce. This has come to an end.' In fact, from 6 May, Northern Ireland was effectively safe because of Hitler's unwise Napoleonic decision to invade Russia in June. There were no more Luftwaffe raids in Ireland except when, inexplicably, German bombs landed in the Fairview and Phoenix Park areas of Dublin, killing thirty people. The folklore of the time claimed that there were long queues at the confessionals in every Catholic church in Dublin. Outside of Belfast the same kind of folklore among nationalists claimed that a pork store in York Street in the city that had placed a sign in its window beside the carcase of a pig saying, 'This pig was cured at Lourdes,' received a direct hit in one of the raids. Those four terrible nights apart the North had, as it was customary to say afterwards, not a bad war.

6

The Welfare State

WAR TENDS TO PRODUCE CHANGE INDEPENDENT of the causes of the conflict. Though Northern Ireland had since its creation been relatively isolated psychologically and intellectually in its depressed provincialism from what later would be known as the 'real world' even its political fastness was not proof against the seismic upheavals that the war produced. The condition of the slum dwellers, thrown into ghastly relief as they fled from the Belfast blitzes, finally convinced the complacent Stormont government that something needed to be done. Many of the refugees were undersized, suffering from malnutrition, lice-infested and tubercular. Their living conditions at home would have disgraced Dickens's London, and parts of Derry were not much better.

Reform socially requires political reforms and that was not going to happen in fortress 'Ulster'. Though there had been some lowering of sectarian watchfulness during the air raids, the tribes involved in their cold war soon retreated behind their entrenchments. Yet the 'new order' and 'fair deal' promised by Andrews in 1941 would seriously have to be considered. These promises were a reactive response to similar reassurances made in the House of Commons by the wartime coalition that included such committed left-wing reformers as Clement Attlee (1883–1967), Ernest Bevin (1881–1951), Sir Stafford Cripps (1889–1952), Hugh Dalton (1887–1962), and Herbert Morrison (1888–1965), among others. The publication in 1942 of the report of William Beveridge (1879–1963) provided a blueprint for what has since been known as the Welfare State and in this matter Northern Ireland had to follow.

Successive Unionist governments had until then resisted 'socialism'. Sir Basil Brooke, who succeeded John Andrews as Prime Minister in 1943, was instinctively right-wing and his approach to planning and the necessary state control was that they would be 'irksome to Ulstermen used to independence'. He was reminded that this 'independence' was funded by the British Treasury. His instincts as a politician were that of minor gentry of the kind that working class Protestants insisted upon electing. Belfast was a large industrial city analogous with Birmingham or Liverpool and should, with universal suffrage, have voted Labour. The class war in Northern Ireland continued to be lateral rather than vertical, the class enemy was not the bosses but the feckless, lazy, clerically manipulated, and intermittently dangerous Fenians. Though there was a considerable amount of debate in the cabinet about whether Northern Ireland should seek independent dominion status like Canada or New Zealand, or be integrated into the United Kingdom like Scotland, Brooke was reconciled to keep its odd devolved status when, after much abrasive negotiation from 1946 on, the Treasury agreed to foot the bill.

The political process in Northern Ireland tends by comparison to make the course of true love seem (*pace* Shakespeare) to run as smooth as on rollerblades. The new health provisions reversed the inter-war situation, bringing down death rates of mothers in childbirth to the statistical norm of the rest of the United Kingdom and generally making the statelet the healthiest part of it. Tuberculosis, the greatest killer of working class children, was virtually eradicated by 1959. The provisions of the National Health

Act were implemented quickly and new teeth and spectacles changed for the better the lives of many old people and children, and increased the prosperity of the burgeoning professions of opticians and dentists.

Yet, because fundamental attitudes rarely change, health provisions brought another fine excuse for sectarian bitterness. The Mater Infirmorum hospital was a voluntary Catholic institution sited at the foot of the Crumlin Road in an essentially Protestant area. It could not come into the National Health Service for fear that under state control its Catholic ethos would be impugned. Unlike similar hospitals in Britain it could not claim state payment for its outpatient services though it continued to provide them free, irrespective of the patients' creeds. Not all Protestants wanted to use the Mater's services. In Brian Moore's autobiographical novel *The Emperor of Ice Cream* (1965) that is set in Belfast during the Blitz a wounded Protestant woman cries, 'Take me to the Royal Victoria, boys!' In the long tradition of Catholic self-help, a group of Belfast businessmen, calling themselves the 'Young Philanthropists', began effective fund-raising mainly by the 'YP' football pools, though they also sponsored cultural events such as visits by professional drama companies and symphony orchestras. It was not until 1972 that the Mater was brought into the health service on acceptable terms.

Education continued to cause trouble. Things were not helped by the appointment of Harry Midgley (1892–1957) as Minister of Education in 1950 by Brooke, now Viscount Brookeborough. Midgley had been a Northern Ireland Labour MP but he lost his seat in Dock Ward in 1938 owing to his noisy public support for Republican Spain during that country's civil war and his public debates with Catholic clergy who defended Franco. He joined the Unionist Party in 1947, writing to Brookeborough on 27 September that he had 'reached the conclusion that there is no room for division among those… who are anxious to preserve the constitutional life and spiritual heritage of our people', and continued to be noted for his virulent anti-Catholicism.

To Catholics his appointment seemed like a calculated snub and even the permanent officials in the ministry deemed it mischievous. Midgley did his best to undo the 1947 Education Act that replicated the act sponsored by 'Rab' Butler (1902–82) in 1944 which proposed free secondary education for all in three types of school – grammar, intermediate and technical – determined by a selection process known since as the 'eleven plus'.[1] It is probably not unjust to suggest that a part of Midgley's opposition lay in the benefits that would accrue to Catholic families on top of family allowance, free health care and free medicines. All the children of Northern Ireland were going to benefit but where were Catholics going to be taught? Lt-Col Samuel Hall-Thompson, the previous minister, had intended to increase capital grants to voluntary schools from 50 to 60 percent, and provide free books, school transport, stationery for all, and school meals for needy children.

There was a considerable delay in the passing of an act that was white-papered in 1946. The objections came from the Churches of all denominations. Catholics regarded the act, which would mean much greater financial pressure on the Church's limited resources, as part of a campaign to make them join the state system. They had the same suspicion about the already offered 'four-and-two' committees, regarding it as 'but an instalment to the complete transfer of our schools'. The Catholic bishops were under a canonical obligation to control education and were prepared to find the money. They felt bitter since Catholics paid the same taxes as the rest but were not given the same financial support. In what was soon to be the Republic of Ireland the Catholic Church was never more dominant and at times northern clerics tended to forget that in Northern Ireland a different situation obtained. Hall-Thompson had much more trouble with the Protestant clergy, who insisted as in 1923 that the state schools should keep their Protestant ethos and demanded religious worship in what should have been secular state schools. Brookeborough betrayed him by attending a meeting in Sandy Row called to protest at his proposal to pay Catholic teachers' national insurance and superannuation. Hall-Thompson resigned but the permanent officials, who were dismayed at the appointment of Midgley, were able to save much of his bill. As a rule the officials acted with scrupulous fairness throughout the whole of Northern Ireland's existence, whatever about the attitudes of their ministers.

The nationalists, now quite disorganised politically in spite of the formation of an Anti-Partition League, felt betrayed again when John A[loysius] Costello (1891–1976), the Taoiseach of the Irish coalition government, announced at a press conference on 7 September 1948 in Ottawa his intention to remove Éire from the Commonwealth and declare it a republic. Under pressure from the Northern Ireland cabinet but with little real reluctance Attlee insisted on 3 May 1949: '…it is hereby affirmed that in no event will Northern Ireland or any part thereof cease to be part of Her Majesty's Dominions and the United Kingdom without the consent of the Parliament of Northern Ireland.' Introducing the bill which became law on 18 August 1949 he observed somewhat ingenuously that he had to 'conclude that the government of Éire considered that the cutting of the last tie which united Éire to the British Commonwealth was a more important objective of policy than ending partition.' He had done nothing to end it himself.

In spite of this further rebuff the nationalists/Catholics of Northern Ireland maintained their customary non-violent constitutionalism. The greater majority were content to wait without relinquishing their anti-partitionist dreams. For one thing their Church had outlawed the IRA, declaring on 18 January 1956 that it was a 'mortal sin for a Catholic to become or remain a member of an organisation or society which arrogates to itself the right to bear arms or to use them against its own or another state; that it is also sinful for a Catholic to co-operate with, express approval of, or otherwise assist any such organisation or society, and that if the cooperation or assistance be notable, the sin committed is mortal'.[2]

Catholics might have argued or grumbled but in those years they followed any hierarchy admonitions.

Most of them were content to wait and make the best of the situation, as they had had to do since 1921. The welfare benefits did make life easier and the appalling problem of housing showed some signs of solution. The setting-up in 1945 of the Northern Ireland Housing Trust by William Grant, the new Minister of Health and Local Government, improved things considerably. Money was supplied on favourable terms by the British Treasury and allocation of houses was scrupulously fair, based upon need and not religion. This was, however, not true of local authorities. Londonderry Corporation did build houses but the ones allocated to Catholics were sited in the overloaded South Ward to continue the necessary gerrymandering. The nationalist council in Newry, to a much smaller extent, were equally partial but in a largely Catholic town. Most councils were, however, Unionist controlled and allocation was partial with Protestant families with few or no children getting preference over large Catholic families. It was such a deliberately partial allocation in the village of Caledon in County Tyrone that led to the first civil rights march, the initial step that led to the domino sequence that brought the conflagration of the 'Troubles' and the fall of Stormont.

Perhaps that fall was inevitable because of built-in structural defects but it is possible that if some charismatic leader, who could have acted independently of the Orange Order and the other vociferous agencies who surged back mentally to the seventeenth century at every suggestion of a gesture to Roman Catholics, had made the necessary moves some form of peaceful coexistence instead of cold war might have been achieved. But none was to be found. The senior cabinet members were elderly and the younger men – often merely junior versions of their leaders – were too ambitious to risk any upset.

In these quiet years there were still possibilities. In the first decade of the state Catholics by their refusal to cooperate with the new system had seemingly externalised themselves. The agreed third of places in the RUC were not subscribed and local franchise and education had gone by default. One reason was the unfounded confidence in the Boundary Commission and the feeling that the system was unsustainable. Another was that Catholics were in a kind of shocked state. They knew better than the government in Dublin what life was like in sectarian six-county Ulster and were appalled at the naivety of Free State officials. Those brave souls who did join the police force or transferred directly from the old RIC did not find working conditions ideal and Catholic officers found it necessary to be more absolute in the discharge of their duties than their Protestant colleagues in case they should be accused of 'favouring their own'. And a career in the Northern Ireland civil service had little to recommend it. As late as 1972, when Stormont fell, only five percent of senior posts were held by Catholics. The population ratio was about 3:7 but the numbers of Catholic company secretaries, university teachers, hospital consultants and registrars, managers and engineers were well below ten percent. Even Catholic GPs formed only a fifth of the medical roster; the highest proportion, at 23 percent, was of members of the legal profession, well below the statistical norm, and may have reflected an age-old love of litigation.

Yet years of seeming acquiescence had created in the nationalist community an alternative and congenial culture. Though by ideological reckoning Catholics were very much an underclass they were treated fairly by government officials if not politicians. On a personal level there were many friendships and lots of acquaintanceship that worked easily enough except at significant dates in the calendar. In nationalist towns like Derry, Strabane, Ballycastle, Downpatrick and Newry, and to a lesser extent Omagh and Dungannon, there was a social life not dissimilar to equivalent towns in the South. Amateur drama and music flourished under the watchful eye of a still authoritarian and paternalistic Church. A lot of activity went into fund-raising to make good the shortfall of government subventions. Nationalists showed themselves fairly tolerant and non-acrimonious except for the flouting of the regulation of public displays of the Irish tricolour, which had hoped to combine orange and green with a neutral white buffer zone. Though naturally sensitive to political slights and local government discrimination in jobs and housing they were essentially a peaceful and not 'disloyal' minority.

The greatest proof of this benignity was shown in the failure of 'Operation Harvest', a border campaign (1956–62) by a resurgent IRA. They had been in great disarray after the bombing campaign in Britain in 1939 largely because of de Valera's policy of internment and ignoring hunger strikes. Sinn Féin had election successes in 1955 when Phil Clarke and Tom Mitchell won seats in Fermanagh–South Tyrone though both were serving ten-year sentences. No Nationalist candidates stood against them and their elections were declared invalid in spite of achieving between them more than 150,000 votes. The leadership took these results as proof of a renewed nationalist commitment to the 'armed struggle' though they were largely sentimental or anti-Unionist votes. Arms had been obtained on 12 June 1954 in a daring raid on the virtually undefended Gough Barracks in Armagh, the headquarters of the Royal Irish Fusiliers. A similar foray into Lisanelly Barracks on 17 October failed and the eight raiders were arrested. On the night of 11–12 December 1956 ten targets were attacked in the North, in Derry, Enniskillen, Magherafelt, Newry, and several bridges in Fermanagh. Among the targets were a BBC transmitter in Rosemount, Derry, the courthouse in Magherafelt, and a B-special hut in Newry. The following night RUC stations in Lisnaskea and Derrylin were unsuccessfully attacked.

The specials were mobilised and many roads into the South, most of them unapproved for vehicle transport, were cratered. The cratering of the most direct road from Derry to Letterkenny was one which caused a great deal of inconvenience as Operation Harvest continued sporadically until 1962. The behaviour of the B-specials on patrol and at checkpoints lived up to the anti-Catholic traditions of the constabulary. If travellers on their way to the second city used the name 'Derry' instead of the officially correct 'Londonderry' they were subject to long irritating delays. Young Catholics were favourite targets for the entirely Protestant force, whose behaviour seemed to be deliberately provocative. Apart from these minor complaints Catholics ignored the campaign. Brian Faulkner (1921–77), the Minister of Home Affairs, one of the few members of the Unionist cabinet with real political talent, interned all known members of the IRA in Northern Ireland. De Valera did the same in the Republic. Eight IRA members, four republican supporters, and six RUC constables were killed. Damage was estimated at one million pounds and the cost of anti-Harvest security measures ten million.

The 'hero' of the campaign, at least the one whose name is best known outside the movement, was Seán South (1929–1957), who was killed with his comrade Fergal O'Hanlon in an unsuccessful attack on Brookeborough barracks early on New Year's Day in 1957. The fact that his Limerick funeral was attended by more than 40,000 people was viewed by northern Unionists as proof that the Republic was full of IRA fellow travellers. They chose to ignore that fact that both Costello and later de Valera moved firmly against the movement with military tribunals and internment. The crowds at the funeral and the swift composing of a celebratory ballad were evidence not of support but of a sentimental feeling for another young death in an apparently hopeless gesture. 'Seán South of Garryowen' joined the already overstocked repertoire of Irish patriotic ballads and the pointless campaign staggered on. In fact there was little real support north and south, and many were hardly aware of the cessation when the IRA called upon its members to dump arms on 26 February 1962. Though Catholics in the North had never relinquished the desire for the reunification of the country they had for many years eschewed any means of attaining this goal other than the wearisome constitutional kind.

Their adversaries never gave them official credit for this stance though Protestant neighbours realised that their Catholic/nationalist acquaintances were far from violent. Even the most sanguine Catholic assenters to the status quo were regularly snubbed in such a way as would have caused Job to lose patience. In 1956 the Minister of Finance, Ivan Neill, brought in a bill to cut off the family allowance to the younger children of large families. There was no suggestion that the measure was directed against Catholic couples, though it was a tenet of Unionist sociological belief that their dysfunction was caused by having too many children. The reason given was good husbandry and fiscal probity. There was immediate protest from Catholics. Even if the suggested change in the social welfare system was not sectarian it was illogical. The larger the family, the greater the need for state assistance. Two Catholic bishops, Neil Farren of Derry and Eugene O'Doherty of Dromore, flew to Westminster to demand the continuation of parity with the British system. On 12 June, after a hurried visit to Downing Street, Brookeborough announced that Northern Ireland would keep pace with Britain, asserting that there was no lapse of principle. He retired as Prime Minister on 25 March 1963.

He must carry some of the responsibility for the catastrophe that followed at the end of the decade. He ruled in an unusually peaceful period when there was no substantial threat to Northern Ireland. He could, perhaps, have prevented the Troubles if he had made any attempt to come to terms with what he regarded as an inherently hostile minority. His successor, Terence O'Neill, saw it a 'tragedy that he did not use his tremendous charm, and his deep Orange roots to try and persuade his devoted followers to accept some reforms'. As O'Neill himself was to discover it was then, to use the recurring cry of the civil rights movement, 'Too little, too late.'

'Too Little, Too Late'

O'NEILL REMAINS SOMETHING OF AN ENIGMA. His CV reads rather more like that of an upper-class Tory that an Ulster Unionist. He was an old Etonian, a captain in the guards and had served during the Second World War (in which his two elder brothers were killed). He was elected Stormont MP for Bannside and continued to represent the constituency until he was defeated by Ian Paisley (1926–) in 1970. He had been Deputy Speaker, Minister of Home Affairs and Minister of Finance. When raised to the peerage as Lord O'Neill of the Maine he seemed quite at home in the House of Lords. Yet his Irish – or rather Anglo-Irish – credentials were impeccable, dating from a provident marriage in the early seventeenth century, and his regiment was the Irish Guards. His accession to the premiership had not been on a vote of the Unionist parliamentary party but rather by oligarchic appointment. He had few social or political skills, suggesting an aristocratic hauteur that he probably did not feel. It was believed by many in the party that Brian Faulkner, a much more able politician, would have been a better choice but there were few precedents. O'Neill was only the fourth Prime Minister in the history of the statelet and he conformed to the pattern of his predecessor Brookeborough and his successor James

Chichester-Clarke (1923–2002), gentry who did their duty. Faulkner, as Lady Bracknell might have put it, did not rise from the ranks of the aristocracy but was born in the purple of commerce and was quite often reminded of it by his grander colleagues, patronised by them as a 'little shirt maker'. It was family rather than talent that won the post for O'Neill.

It is interesting if ultimately pointless to consider what kind of leader Faulkner might have made if appointed then. He was an enthusiastic Orangeman but later proved sufficiently pragmatic to accept the post of Chief Executive of the power-sharing assembly. His appointment as Minister of Commerce was one of O'Neill's smarter decisions since he proved adept at obtaining foreign investment and undoubtedly made a major contribution to Northern Ireland's significant prosperity in the 1960s. He was probably less aware of the need to try to conciliate Catholic/nationalist feelings than O'Neill though even now it is hard to decide whether the latter's gestures were caused by a genuine awareness of injustices and the need to assuage them or by a judicious feeling that something had to be done to prevent some kind of dangerous revolt. O'Neill tended to be impulsive and act without consultation. His sensational meeting with Sean Lemass (1899–1971), the Irish Taoiseach, on 14 January 1965, was a surprise to many colleagues. It was a courageous act, even if its main purpose was to look for greater economic cooperation. Lemass, in fact, had more to lose since his travelling to meet the Prime Minister of Northern Ireland gave de facto recognition for the first time to the lost counties. The meeting, which took place in Stormont was, if nothing else, evidence of a thaw and it was followed by a further meeting in Dublin on 9 February. One week before in a token of rapprochement 'Big Eddie' McAteer (1914–86), the Nationalist leader, agreed to make his party the official opposition at Stormont.

The Northern Ireland Labour Party (NILP) had suffered an eclipse after the publication in 1965 by O'Neill of his manifesto in which he announced that he intended to create new jobs and prepare with houses for an expected increase in population. It pulled their reforming carpet from under them. Throughout the whole history of Northern Ireland, Unionist fears of socialism were even greater than that of nationalism. They feared that with a strong labour party the Protestant vote might be split, making the Unionist Party vulnerable to a coalition of non-Unionists. In the 1965 Stormont general election their fears proved false. Thirty-six Unionists were returned, Nationalists had their usual nine but the NILP, which had won four seats in the 1962 election, had that number reduced to two. The occlusion of the NILP was the most successful – perhaps the only unalloyed successful – achievement of the O'Neill era.

It was noticed that most of the new employment ventures were sited in Unionist areas like Carrickfergus, Antrim, Ballymena and Coleraine, all east of the Bann river that divides Northern Ireland from north to south. West of the Bann, in the counties of Tyrone and Fermanagh, and the Maiden City, Catholics were just a majority. No one west of the Bann was surprised that of the two railways, LMS and GNR, the one closed down in 1963 for 'rationalisation' was the GNR (beyond loyal Portadown) which linked Derry, Strabane and Dungannon, and connected the west to Dublin, and not the LMS which served loyal north Derry and Antrim. Apologists argued that the report on railway viability had recommended the closing of both railway systems but this did not in any way weaken the argument that it was the west that was made to suffer.

There *was* surprise and anger when the Lockwood Report in 1965 recommended that the second university should go to Coleraine, a small prosperous Protestant town, instead of Derry, a city with a population five times as large and economically depressed, that already had a nucleus in Magee College. The decision then, and now, seems bizarre. Defenders of Lockwood (which incidentally had not a single Catholic member and few Irish people) claim that it was because there was more room for expansion on the Coleraine site. The present day expansion of Magee makes nonsense of that argument. There still seems no explanation but the political one that a nationalist city like Derry was only going to get the crumbs that fell from the east's table. A motorcade, involving 25,000 people, organised by the University for Derry Action Committee (UDAC), drove the seventy-six miles from Derry to Stormont on 18 February 1965. They thronged the parkland grounds of Stormont, surrounding the minatory statue of Carson, and led by Albert Anderson, the Unionist mayor of the city, and the leader of his apparently permanent opposition, 'Big Eddie'. There was disappointment and even greater anger when, after the award of the university to Coleraine, it was discovered that seven members of the Londonderry Unionist Association, known locally as the 'nameless faceless men' (though everybody knew their names) had tried to influence the committee and at least three of them had been on the motorcade. Derry nationalists were being taught a sharp lesson in *realpolitik*. The organiser of the protest was John Hume (1937–), a dynamic and charismatic natural leader who had been a teacher of French and had begun a career of public service, working with the Credit Union movement and local rent-to-buy housing. He was to play an important part in the future history not only of his native town of Derry but of Northern Ireland as a whole.

A promised new town, named with exquisite tact Craigavon, was created near solid Portadown, rather than follow its planner's suggestion of developing Derry. The work was in the charge of the Minister of Development, William Craig (1924–2011), who as Minister of Home Affairs had a significant part in government response to the civil rights agitation. The name of the new bridge over the Lagan in Belfast was to be Carson, an example of further ecumenical tact, until Lord Wakehurst, the governor-general, the queen's representative in Northern Ireland, stepped in and decreed that the bridge be called the Queen Elizabeth Bridge, a not much better title and leaving Belfast with two bridges twenty yards apart called the Queen Elizabeth and the Queen's.

Then in 1966 the Derry naval base, the source of some work and (with regular visits of NATO ships) entertainment for the beleaguered city, was shut down. It was part, said the Admiralty with a perceptible shrug, of a general cutback in naval expenditure. There was little complaint from Stormont. Nationalists of west Ulster took the disappointments with their usual lack of surprise and all except a few diehards exonerated O'Neill from absolute blame. One wit from Derry, when it was manifest that the area west of the Bann was not going to have the same advantages of the east, said that the motto for protestors should be 'Bomb the Bann', a nice inversion of the contemporary Campaign for Nuclear Disarmament (CND) cry, 'Ban the Bomb'.

The decade of the 1960s was different from that of the 1920s and certainly the 1930s. Because of the safety net of the Welfare State life was easier. The 1947 Education Act, which provided generous grants for those who wished to attend universities or polytechnics, had produced a generation of young graduates, better educated than their parents and unlike them impatient of the political climate of Northern Ireland. John Hume and Bernadette Devlin (1947–) were typical of a new breed of nationalists who understood what was happening in the North and anxious, if in different ways, to change things for the better. They were aware too of radical movements elsewhere, in the southern states of America, in South Africa where the remote beginnings of the end of apartheid were just visible and, towards the end of the decade, in Prague. They turned a critical eye too on what they still called the 'Free State', objecting to what they perceived as undue clerical influence, the cagy protectionism of the de Valera era, and such measures as the Censorship of Publications legislation. Yet in spite of that cold eye they tended to identify with 'free' Ireland and have no real empathy with the 'Six Counties' even though they lived their lives there.

Even older people could not but be affected by the 'swinging

Sixties'. RTÉ television was added to the BBC and Ulster Television (UTV) in making people aware of life outside the truncated province. The Second Vatican Council (1962–5), called by the 'caretaker' Pope John XXIII (1881–1963), had effects well beyond the Church. The election of John F Kennedy (1917–63) as the first Irish-American Catholic president of the United States in 1960 and his visit to Ireland in 1963 (that did not include a trip north) gave nationalists a sense of wider belonging. There was in the air a palpable sense of change and the possibility of improvement. If not exactly the Wordsworthian, 'Bliss was it that dawn to be alive', to be young was very heaven as proved by beehive hairstyles, hot pants, Carnaby Street, and the pop music explosion led by The Beatles and the extremes (as it seemed to elders) of Woodstock. Even so hermetically sealed a society could not withstand the relentless media pressure. For the first time since the bleak days of 1921 the South was buoyant and the North was lagging behind socially and psychologically.

O'Neill's gestures to Catholics, visiting Catholic schools, shaking hands with priests, offering sympathy to Cardinal William Conway (1913–77) when John XXIII died were looked at with mild interest by Catholics but with growing suspicion by grassroots Protestants. They had found a new champion in the Rev Dr Ian Richard Kyle Paisley. Ordained by his Baptist father in 1946 he founded his own denomination, the Free Presbyterian Church of Ulster, in 1951. Until 1964 his political activities were low-key, consisting mainly of eloquent and vituperative denunciation of any kind of compromise with extreme Unionism in his Belfast church, 'Martyrs Memorial', and in his newspaper, the *Protestant Telegraph*, that was also used for vociferous denunciation of the Catholic Church, especially its current leader whom he characterised as 'Old Redsocks'. He was tall, strong and loudly effective in the rhetoric of attack, and soon saw O'Neill as an enemy of the people.

Paisley's first star appearance was during the 1964 Westminster general election when during the campaign Jim Kilfedder (1928–

95) – later Sir James (1994) – was standing in West Belfast. Paisley heard that a small Irish tricolour was displayed in the window of the Republican office in Divis Street, the link of the Falls Road to the city centre.[1] He threatened to bring enough of his followers to remove it if the authorities did not. It was removed by the RUC under the problematic Flags and Emblems Act. There was some trouble with the totally Catholic inhabitants. A few nights later, on 1 October, another tricolour appeared in the office and the police used pickaxes to break the door down to remove it. The riots that followed lasted two days with stones, petrol bombs, water cannon, burning vehicles, including a bus, and sirens wailing reminding older people of the civic trouble in 1935. It was also a 'coming attraction' trailer for many similar confrontations with the RUC facing the nationalists as if to defend the Protestants. Kilfedder won the election and thanked Paisley for his help, without which he might have failed.

Paisley's reputation as a rabble-rouser had already been established. In 1958 he had accused the Queen Mother and Princess Margaret of 'spiritual fornication and adultery with the Antichrist' because they had visited John XXIII and when the pope died he caused bewildered rage when he reassured an audience in the Ulster Hall, 'This Romish man of sin is now in Hell.' On 6 June 1966, after a demonstration at the Presbyterian General Assembly, his march through Cromac Street in the Catholic Markets area caused rioting and he was arrested. On 19 July refusing to promise to keep the peace he was imprisoned for three months, achieving the martyr status that is almost an essential part of the CV of any Irish political leader. Now conscious of the spirit of the times he sensed danger and placed the blame squarely on the shoulders of O'Neill. He pursued him on every possible occasion, finally being elected in 1970 in O'Neill's own constituency of Bannside. Paisley knew how to deal with nationalists but probably regarded O'Neill as Unionism's main enemy. It became clear in the second half of the decade that Paisley spoke for many who had hitherto automatically supported official Unionist candidates. None had the rhetorical power or the instinct to understand the psyche of grassroots Protestantism. His popularity and power grew after every confrontation with O'Neillism so that by the end of the troubled century he was to emerge as the representative and the voice of the people beset by the bogeymen of Catholicism and, as they saw it, in spite of the denunciation of the Catholic clergy, its military arm, the IRA.

A few of those he unofficially spoke for, probably feeling the same fear of the possible dissolution of Protestant ascendancy, exhumed the Ulster Volunteer Force (UVF) that was going to fight and be right in 1913. They were also prompted in their actions by enthusiastic celebrations of the fiftieth anniversary of the Easter Rising of 1916 in the North. The Protestant mythology associated 1916 with the slaughter of the 36th (Ulster) Division at the Ancre in the Battle of the Somme in July, a blood sacrifice for king and country, in marked contrast to the 'stab-in-the-back' actions of the rebels two months earlier. They made a formal declaration of war on the IRA, then virtually non-existent. The simplistic equation 'Catholic = IRA supporter' led to attacks on Catholic property and the deaths of two Catholics, John Scullion in Clonard Street, off the Falls Road, on 27 May, and Peter Ward in Malvern Street at the foot of the Shankill on 26 June. Two other Catholics who were shot with Ward survived.

O'Neill, hearing of the murders, declared the UVF illegal, stating on 28 June: 'This evil thing in our midst… now takes its place alongside the IRA in the schedule of illegal bodies.' They had their revenge with explosions in electrical sub-stations in Belfast in March, post offices and buses set on fire on the Falls Road, and an explosion at the Silent Valley reservoir cutting off a large amount of Belfast's water supply. Ironically the IRA was blamed but the outrages had the desired effect: O'Neill resigned as leader and the North headed resolutely into its Troubles.

Though O'Neill lacked the more obvious political gifts he seemed honest and genuinely interested in reform. If any of the previous prime ministers, especially Craigavon, had made the gestures that characterised the first years of his premiership the effect might have been remarkable. Certainly the beleaguered nationalists, betrayed and in disarray after the Boundary Commission's flop, might then have been grateful for the reform that he attempted, however slow and at times mishandled.

The nationalists of the 1960s were a different breed. They were more articulate and, though still discriminated against, better off socially and financially. They benefited, as we have seen, from the welfare provisions – some Unionists believed disproportionately. Since emigration was not the imperative it had been before the increased buoyancy of the economy there were more young people able to stay and, it was believed in certain circles, make trouble. They grew impatient not only with the painfully slow pace of reform but also with what they saw as stodgy Nationalist politics. It is a demographic cliché – and therefore true – that when reform occurs in an unjust regime the government is in a situation most perilous, as Hercule Poirot might put it. The usual authority for this tenet is the French political philosopher, Alexis de Tocqueville (1805–59), who wrote in his magisterial work, *L'ancien regime* (1856), '…experience shows that the most dangerous moment for a bad government is generally that in which it sets about reform'.

A vocal and educated nationalist population was in no way anxious to bring down the regime by violence but they were prepared to be vigorously constitutional in a campaign for reform. One glaring example of injustice was in local council housing where, in a large majority of places, Catholics were sorely discriminated against. In May 1963 a group of Catholic Dungannon housewives formed the Homeless Citizens League (HCL) and petitioned the gerrymandered Dungannon Urban Council with proof that while they had to live in overcrowded squalor, Protestants, some not even from the area, were being accommodated immediately. Out of this small group grew the Campaign for Social Justice (CSJ) that began its existence on 17 January 1964 in Belfast, though its two most visible members were Dr Conn and Patricia McCluskey who had been important members of the HCL. It was they who coined the now non-PC battle cry, 'One man – One vote', that became one of the causes fought for by the composite movement, the Northern Ireland Civil Rights Association (NICRA). The cry referred to the multiple or company votes that, with ward-rigging, maintained, as in Derry, a Unionist minority in power.

As civil rights agitation grew more successful it seemed a logical development to form NICRA. Unionists claimed that it was merely a blanket title for the IRA and its fellow travellers. There were indeed some members of a slowly renascent IRA under NICRA's umbrella but there were also communists, academics with no obvious political alliance, old fashioned AOH nationalists, even a few independently minded Protestants, but mainly a new generation of activists who were imbued with the free protesting spirit of the 'wonderful decade' who could give detailed accounts of Martin Luther King's (1929–68) successful civil rights campaigns and mourned his recent and not entirely unexpected death on 4 April 1968. One radical group that was part of NICRA was the nucleus of People's Democracy (PD), originating in the usually apolitical Queen's University of Belfast (QUB) and destined to figure prominently in Northern Ireland affairs early in the following year.

In June 1968 the young Austin Currie (1939–), who had been elected MP for East Tyrone in 1964, engaged in a copybook piece of the 'direct action' that NICRA had promised against a copybook piece of the injustice it sought to highlight. On the twentieth of that month he squatted in a house in the Tyrone village of Caledon that had been allocated to an unmarried Protestant woman, the nineteen-year-old Emily Beattie, secretary to a local Unionist candidate.[2] It was too blatant an example of queue jumping to be allowed to pass without comment. Marches had worked in Mississippi, so why not in Tyrone.

On 24 August NICRA called Ireland's first civil rights march from Coalisland to Dungannon. It was a distance of five miles and all passed peacefully until the 2,500 participants reached the outskirts of Dungannon where they were met with 400 RUC men with dogs and a makeshift barricade of ropes slung between three tenders. Paisley's band of followers, the Ulster Protestant Volunteers (UPV), had organised a counter-demonstration and had taken over the Market Square. In the pattern of many similar confrontations the RUC stood with their backs to the Protestants and faced the NICRA marchers. The latter were persuaded to disperse quietly to emphasise that they were 'a peaceful people asking for our civil rights in an orderly manner'. Before the crowd dispersed they condemned the RUC for stopping a legal march and William Craig, the truculent Minister of Home Affairs.

In the weeks that followed the Derry Housing Action Committee (DHAC), organised by Eamonn McCann (1943–) and Eamon Melaugh, laid plans for the next march to be held in the Maiden City on 5 October. Craig banned the march using as his excuse that a 'traditional' Apprentice Boys of Derry march was to take place at the same time.[3] Many members of NICRA wanted to cancel the march that would follow what had been a traditional route for the Apprentice Boys. DHAC members insisted that the protest should go ahead. Among the leaders was Gerry Fitt (1926–2005), later Lord Fitt of Bell's Hill, who, elected for West Belfast in 1966, had enlightened the House of Commons about the true state of Northern Ireland. He was accompanied by three Labour MPs who had come straight from the Labour Party Conference. Fitt and 'Big Eddie' were struck on the head by police batons, others in equally sensitive and more painful places. Fitt's bloodied face was seen by world television and the authorities' means of dealing with protest that had been a commonplace since 1921 was revealed in all its one-sided nastiness. Batons, boots and water cannon were used indiscriminately against protestors and onlookers alike, and all was recorded by television cameras, especially those of RTÉ. People who had not attended the march but had heard the details commented, 'So it has started, then!' It had. The RUC's attack was followed by two nights of rioting – and looting – setting the pattern for many similar nights and days of urban violence.

Harold Wilson (1916–95), the prime minister, and James Callaghan (1912–2005), the Home Secretary, were extremely embarrassed about the UK's guilty secret being made public. O'Neill, Craig and Faulkner were summoned to Downing Street on 4 November and ordered to put their house in order. The meeting resulted in the announcement on 22 November which granted nearly all of NICRA's demanded reforms, including a points system for housing allocation, the appointment of an ombudsman, an end to multiple votes, a review of the draconian Special Powers Act, and the replacement of the gerrymandered, permanently Unionist, Londonderry Corporation by a commission. It was not enough; for the first time, but not the last, the cry 'Too little, too late' was heard. On 9 December O'Neill went on television to give his 'crossroads' talk:

> Ulster stands at the crossroads... There are, I know, today some so-called loyalists who talk of independence from Britain – who seem to want a kind of Protestant Sinn Féin. Rhodesia in defying Britain at least has an air force and an army of her own. Where are the Ulster armoured divisions and the Ulster jet planes? ...Unionism armed with justice will be a stronger cause than Unionism armed merely with strength... What kind of Ulster do you want? A happy and respected province in good standing with the rest of the United Kingdom? Or a place continually torn apart by riots and demonstrations?

The speech generated 150,000 letters of support and Northern Ireland had a peaceful Christmas. The writers of all those letters either chose to ignore or missed the double-think of the talk. Only the wisest prophets – or the most ambitious – knew that it was only the end of the first act of the long, long drama and they correctly interpreted O'Neill's sacking of William Craig from the cabinet on 11 December. His letter to Craig gave as the chief reason, 'I have known for some time that you were attracted by the idea of a UDI [Unilateral Declaration of Independence, as in Southern Rhodesia] nature... clearly you cannot propose such views and stay in the government.' Though the move pleased nationalists who disliked Craig as much for his abrasiveness as for his blanket bans on 'non-traditional' marches, it was an act through which O'Neill had increased the enmity of one of his former friends.

8

Lighting the Fuse

THE PEACEFUL CHRISTMAS DWINDLED INTO A turbulent New Year. On the Wednesday after the 5 October march in Derry around 3,000 QUB students with some twenty members of the academic staff marched to the City Hall in Belfast – or rather failed to reach the City Hall because some of the group led by Paisley who had caused them to avoid the direct route through Shaftesbury Square, which he filled with counter-demonstrators, had planted themselves round the City Hall, and the RUC, as usual, had made no effort to move them. They sat in the rain for three hours making a peaceful protest and when they returned to Queen's formed an action group called People's Democracy (PD).

Paisley was to continue disruption of all civil rights events, as in Armagh on 30 November when 6,000 were prevented from entering the centre of the city because a band of Paisleyites had occupied it during the night. Apprised that his assembly was illegal Paisley said he was holding a religious service. Even the RUC were surprised at this, considering that they had confiscated guns, scythes and billhooks from supporters arriving in mid-morning. Again the marchers faced by the police acquiesced and, apart from an attack on an ITN cameraman by a loyalist wielding a lead-filled stocking, the day passed peacefully.

Some undergraduate members of the PD refused to accept that enough had been gained by 'O'Neill's miserable reforms', as Michael Farrell, one of the group, described them. He, Bernadette Devlin, and more than thirty others decided to hold a 'long march' of seventy-five miles from Belfast to Derry, requiring more than had been offered. Most members of NICRA (even of the PD) were against it, including 'Big Eddie' and John Hume who felt that the choreography was wrong. Still they marched, avoiding with difficulty and re-routings set pieces of antagonism from Paisleyites who had harassed them from the outset when they began their journey at 9am on New Year's Day 1969. The march was legal – O'Neill refused to ban it – so the students were under the grudging protection of the RUC, or so they thought. On 3 January Major Ronald Bunting (1924–84), then an ally of Paisley and arrested with him for their participation in the Armagh disruption on 30 November, announced that he had 'given a request to the loyal citizens of Ulster and, thank God, they have responded to hinder and harry it [the 'long march'] and I think they've hindered it and, I think you will agree, to a certain extent they have harried it'.

On the morning of 4 January the marchers left the village of Claudy and headed down the main road to Derry. They were joined by some supporters and numbered seventy by the time they reached Burntollet Bridge, about eight miles from their destination. They were advised by the RUC that a gang was gathered in nearby fields but they accepted the police assurance that they might just manage to get through. That was the impression the marchers gained but in fact they were being led into a well-organised ambush. Some loads of newly quarried stones had thoughtfully been delivered to the site and crates of empty bottles were bussed in. The marchers were hailed with these bottles and stones. When some tried to escape into the fields nearby they were driven back on to the road by policemen using batons. Some of the assailants were identified as local members of the B-specials. Many were injured and even the walking wounded were again attacked as they passed the Protestant Irish Street estate on the outskirts of the city where, as the press reported, the adults were urging their children to throw stones. The marchers, including a bandaged and bloody Bernadette Devlin, were given a rapturous reception in Guildhall Square.

Darkness comes early in Derry in January and as night fell the RUC attacked shoppers in a city centre store and smashed glass counters. Later that night the RUC Reserve invaded the Bogside, a nationalist part of town, taking its name from a street that preserved a geological memory of the ancient city. They turned on people in the streets, throwing stones and attacking buildings, including the new offices of the Credit Union. That night 'Free Derry' was born. The words 'You are now entering Free Derry' appeared on Sunday, 5 January on the gable of a house in St Columb's Wells. The words presaged the 'no-go' area that the Bogside was to become on 12 August. Though the house has disappeared the gable-end stands free, a permanent symbol of defiance.

O'Neill made a blustering attempt to put all the blame on the young marchers but journalists in the posh papers and television pictures told a different story. Up till that moment the RUC as a force had been again getting a sort of acceptance by the nationalist community but now they were totally execrated. The ferocity of some of their members that night in Derry had a kind of millennial temper as though they instinctively believed that this was the end or the beginning of something in the North. O'Neill was again summoned to Downing Street and shortly afterwards announced the setting up of a commission under Lord Cameron, a Scottish judge, and having as one of its members J J Campbell, who as 'Ultach' had excoriated the Unionist government in the 1930s.

Bernadette Devlin had felt exhilarated when she arrived in Derry after the march, writing in her autobiography, *The Price of My Soul* (1969), 'the war was over and we had won; we hadn't lifted a finger but we had won'. Certainly the PD march had weakened O'Neill's position. Faulkner had resigned because of the Cameron Commission, calling it 'an abdication of authority', and the giant menacing form of Paisley must have seemed to O'Neill to blot out the light.

The spring came, surely the most eventful in the history of Northern Ireland. Soon after Easter John Hume, Paddy Devlin, Ivan Cooper and Paddy O'Hanlon were Stormont MPs and Bernadette Devlin had been elected to Westminster as its youngest ever MP. The UVF reservoir explosions 'blew me out of office', as the late prime minister afterwards recorded. There had been a change too in NICRA; moderates like the McCluskeys resigned, correctly forecasting that Republican militants had obtained a significant voice in the association. Republicans had had an adage for many years: 'England's difficulty; Ireland's opportunity.' Since Fenian times or even earlier the 'armed struggle' had been part of Republican mythology as the only reliable means of defeating the British. Now smarting from the failure of Operation Harvest they began to regroup and the month of December 1969 was to see a split in their ranks into the 'Official' IRA, known as 'Stickies', and the more militant, rather right-wing group called 'Provisional', who remained obstinately abstentionist in opposition to the Officials who had had some aspirations to constitutional, if rather radical, politics.[1] The Official IRA declared a ceasefire in May 1970 after a number of atrocities that they claimed weakened their cause but the Provos (or Provies), as they soon came to be called, continued their campaign until 1994. The reinvigorated IRA was a product of the end of the year 1969; their reputation at the end of the summer was quite low.

O'Neill found it wise to resign on 28 April after a snap election called in February gave him no comfort. He was replaced by his doppelganger Chichester-Clarke who had the same gentry background. During his period in power protest marches continued even though the principle of 'One man – one vote' had been established. After a banned NICRA march in Derry on 19 April that was followed by serious rioting eight uniformed RUC officers burst into the home of Samuel Devenny (1927–69) and severely batoned him and some friends who were in the house. His death three months later of a heart condition was attributed to the incident. Sir Arthur Young (1908–79), appointed chief constable of the RUC in August by James Callaghan, found that during his investigation in 1970 he was met by a conspiracy of silence and no one was ever charged. Others escaped sanctions when Chichester-Clarke declared an amnesty for anyone charged or convicted for public order offences since October 1968. The Devenny case gave one more reason for distrust of the RUC; the B-specials had been discredited in nationalist eyes for decades. It also increased the already tense situation as the spring became the long hot summer of the marching season. Nationalist areas throughout the North became accustomed to the noxious fumes of CS gas and young rioters eventually reached the stage of manual dexterity that enabled the deft to actually catch rubber bullets in flight.

July came with the chief Orange celebration of the 'glorious, pious and immortal memory' of William of Orange who confirmed his right to the title William III by defeating James II in 1690. The iconic Battle of the Boyne was fought on 1 July but the calendar revision placed its anniversary on the 'Twelfth', which is celebrated with costume, march, speech and music all over Northern Ireland. For the first time in thirty years it was characterised by riots, attacks on the now sorely stretched police force, and on the nationalist enclave of Unity Flats at the foot of the Protestant Shankill Road. There was trouble in Dungiven and Derry but what people dreaded was the Apprentice Boys of Derry's celebration of the end of the famous siege in 1689. The society had been founded in 1814 in token to the thirteen London apprentices who had symbolically shut the Ferryquay gate against the Jacobite troops of Lord Antrim in December 1688. Their day was the other 'Twelfth', 12 August, and the ritual included a circuit of the carriageway on top of the city's walls. Trouble was almost a certainty considering the temper of Derry nationalists, especially those who lived under the west wall. In the past they had greeted the marchers with black smoke from their chimneys.

John Hume travelled to London to try to persuade the Home Office to have the march called off. Robert Porter, the Minister of Home Affairs, who replaced Craig, had been reluctant to cancel knowing how loyalists reacted when such threats had been made in the past. Some Bogside residents formed the Derry Citizens Defence Association (DCDA) led by an IRA veteran Sean Keenan, and petrol bombs and heaps of stones were stockpiled against a possible irruption of RUC as had occurred after Burntollet and in April. One of the stories of the time concerns a note left for a milkman: 'No milk but leave 200 bottles.'

The day's events were almost over when trouble began. It was said that some of the marchers had tossed pennies down from the walls; others claimed that nationalist youths had thrown stones at the marchers. Whatever the spark the Battle of the Bogside began not long after five o'clock on the evening of 12 August and lasted until about the same time on the fourteenth. During those forty-eight hours much had happened elsewhere.

Jack Lynch, the Irish Taoiseach, broadcast on television on the evening of the thirteenth to announce that since the Stormont government had lost control the Irish government would not stand by while innocent people were in danger of injury or worse. He intended to set up field hospitals just across the border, a mere three miles away at its nearest point. He did not intend to allow the Irish army to cross the border for fear of even greater violence shown to the already beleaguered Catholics in nationalist areas of Belfast. He urged instead the setting up of a United Nations peacekeeping force. The decision not to send troops disappointed some members of his own party and was a sore blow to the Bogside defenders who had hoped that this was to be the battle that would begin the process of Irish reunification.

The call by the DCDA to nationalists about the North to show support to the Derry resistance had dire effects in Belfast. It was interpreted incorrectly by Unionists as a general call for insurrection. Their age-old terror had finally come to pass and they showed the same visceral response as in 1912 – and 1688. The trouble with visceral responses is that they are physical and not mental. Logic and selectivity play little part. All Catholics were the enemy and the actions of hooligans on both sides made the old enmity lethal. The Catholics of Bombay Street between the Falls and the Shankill were literally burnt out of their houses. There was also the same kind of murderous violence in the Ardoyne. The IRA, later regarded as the defenders of Catholic Belfast, were barely organised. The writing on the wall read 'IRA – I ran away' but those August nights made the people psychologically dependent on their defenders and explained the consistent support of the Provos in the areas where the RUC, in a kind of desperation, fired Browning machine guns at the Catholic high-rise Divis flats killing a nine-year-old boy. The tribunal set up under Lord Scarman (1911–2004) to investigate the violence of that summer found that ten people had died, 154 were wounded by gunfire, and 745 injured. The first fatality of the Troubles was John Gallagher who had been shot when B-specials had fired into a crowd during a riot after a civil rights demonstration in Armagh. There were also violent scenes in Dungiven, Dungannon and Newry.

In Derry many very young people were involved in the Bogside battle, impervious to the noxious CS gas and still ready to pour petrol into bottles for stronger arms to throw at policemen. The mythology of the time asserts that around six o'clock in the evening there was a lull when the youngsters of Creggan, a nationalist housing estate also successfully barricaded, went home for tea. One local dairy lost more than 40,000 bottles that were used for other purposes.

By 5pm on 14 August the RUC were totally exhausted and still unable to penetrate the Bogside defences. James Callaghan received a request for troops while returning by plane from a holiday in Cornwall and pressed the necessary buttons. Soldiers of the Prince of Wales' Own Regiment entered the Bogside and took over the duty of security from the spent RUC personnel.

That night saw some of the worst violence perpetrated by the well-armed UVF against Catholics in the Falls Road and Ardoyne. The few IRA guns were no match and the RUC either feared to try to stop the attacks or were not able. Pleas from Ardoyne priests eventually persuaded Callaghan to send the troops into Belfast as well. At about 4 o'clock on the afternoon of 15 August, soldiers of the 2nd Battalion of the Queen's Regiment took over from the RUC to general nationalist rejoicing. They were followed by troops of the Royal Regiment of Wales. They took some time to find their bearings about the city they scarcely knew and there was further violence that night and on the Saturday. Full of tea offered by housewives in the Bogside and nationalist areas of Belfast the soldiers were surprised at their warm reception and for some time they were feted, especially in Derry. The prophetic admonition of Lieutenant-General Sir Ian Freeland, the British army's GOC, 'Honeymoons can be very short-lived,' made on Monday, 18 August, was not heeded and that Christmas children of all persuasions were entertained by the military at parties in camps and barracks.

Unionists were for a time sorely dismayed. They felt that they were defenceless (apart from the very able UVF) with the RUC disarmed and the B-specials stood down. When it became clear that the latter were to be disbanded a crowd marched down the Shankill towards the nationalist Unity Flats on 11 October. When the army intervened there was a riot in which, early next morning, Constable Victor Arbuckle was killed, the first fatality of the renewed violence, shot by the UVF. Two civilians were killed by the army and sixty-six wounded. It seemed that the UVF had met a superior force and that any confrontation would be with Unionists and not, as might be expected, with nationalists. For a while the army seemed to favour the latter but this was an aberration. Already the officers were being entertained in the great houses of the Protestant gentry and told the true 'facts' of the situation. Euphoria remained high, however, in nationalist areas. Jim Callaghan had come to Belfast on 27 August and Derry on the twentieth-eighth. He was received rapturously in the Bogside, attended by John Hume, and spoke with a megaphone from an upstairs window, assuring the densely packed crowds that he was not neutral but on the side of all people who were deprived of justice. He had crossed the painted white lines that marked the edge of the 'no-go area' that the Bogside had become.

He returned on 12 October, bringing with him Sir Arthur Young to become the new head of the RUC and implement the recommendations of the Hunt report, which caused the Shankill riots the same day. Things had worked out better than nationalists had ever dared hope but now a new ingredient had been added to the mixture. PIRA, as the Provisionals now called themselves with the fondness for acronymic labelling that characterised both sides in the struggle, had agreed to begin the long war that would surely lead to the desired reunification of the country. They heard again ancestral voices prophesying war. Their authority for waging such a war with inevitable civilian casualties may be found in the opening words of the Fenian oath administered in the 1860s: 'I do solemnly swear allegiance to the Irish Republic, now virtually established…' Its legality seems to many utterly specious but the rest of the oath with its promises 'to take up arms at moment's notice' and 'to yield absolute obedience to the commands of my superior officers' were assented to by many young, mainly working class people in the years 1970–3 as the crude ham-fisted action of the authorities acted unwittingly as recruiting drives. The government officials, the army, the RUC, and the Ulster Defence Regiment (UDR) that replaced the B-specials on 1 April 1970, all seemed to the IRA to be the means of perpetuating the partition of the country and so were regarded as 'legitimate targets'. No one seemed to understand the determination of IRA recruits or their courage. In nationalist areas where unemployment rates were high it provided a structure and purpose to their lives. Gone were the Marxist tendencies; instead the PIRA emerged as traditionalist, right-wing, and perhaps even fascist, as some of its detractors claimed. Their support by their communities was based on the belief that they were the only defence against the UVF and, from August 1971, the Ulster Defence Association (UDA), the RUC, and the BA (British army), as the once welcome soldiers came to be called. The peace lines in Belfast were not simple white marks on the link roads that led, say, from the Falls to the Shankill, but high wire fences set in concrete.

The first action by the security forces that increased enrolment in the PIRA was the illegal, no-warning curfew imposed on the Lower Falls on 3 July 1970. It lasted thirty-five hours, during which there was no means of obtaining food and 20,000 people, including children, were kept confined while 5,000 homes were searched with much damage to property. A Conservative government had won power under the leadership of the insensitive Edward Heath (1916– 2005) and this action was seen as indicating his government's attitude to the Northern Ireland troubles. In the rioting that followed six civilians were killed. The military's incursions earned them over 100 guns, 100 home-made bombs, 250lbs of explosives, 20,000 rounds of ammunition, and the undying hatred of the people of the time and that of the next generation. The Falls Road residents accused the soldiers of unnecessary violence and looting, which was denied by Freeland, and advised them that should they have replicated the curfew and searches in the Shankill they would have had much richer pickings.

The arrest and imprisonment of Bernadette Devlin for her part in the defence of the Bogside was a further example of Heath's small-mindedness. The absolute end of the honeymoon had been anticipated on 27 June in the isolated, nationalist Short Strand area of east Belfast, the scene of old violence. As a loyalist force converged on St Matthew's Church the army claimed they could do nothing but close off the Lagan bridges. The PIRA began shooting at the loyalist force, killing six people and losing one of their own men. It was to be followed by many other attacks throughout the North. The first British soldier was killed on 6 February 1971 during rioting in the New Lodge Road area. On 10 March three off-duty soldiers were found shot dead in the Ligoniel area of Belfast, lured there, it was believed, by women.

Rioting and bombing became a part of the daily life in parts of Belfast and Derry, and intermittently in other parts of the North. The ecstatic welcome for local heroine Dana (1951–) in March 1970 when she won the Eurovision Song Contest degenerated into a riot. In spite of this life continued with remarkable zest. Adrenalin levels were high and amateur music and drama flourished. In such colleges as the Rupert Stanley in Belfast and the Institute of Continuing Education in Derry foundation courses were overbooked. People got quickly used to the new decimal coinage, introduced on 15 February 1971, and bade farewell to the 'make', the 'wing', the 'bob', the 'half-dollar', and the 'ten-bob note' (slang terms that had been used for 150 years) and learnt to use the letter 'p' instead of 'd' when stating amounts in pence. It was introduced in the South on the same day and one old Kerry woman, interviewed by an RTÉ radio reporter, insisted it would 'never catch on here'.

Television and radio coverage brought the growing Troubles into living rooms throughout Northern Ireland, many who could receive it preferring to view the extensive coverage provided by RTÉ. There was everywhere a mixture of foreboding and exhilaration that is characteristic of living in interesting times when one is conscious of experiencing history at first hand. As time passed a certain euphoria leached away and the facts of the Troubles became tolerated, if hardly welcome. The Conservative Home Secretary, Reginald Maudling

(1917–79), came in for a great deal of criticism for his resigned statement on 15 December:

> I don't think one can speak of defeating the IRA, of eliminating them completely, but it is the design of the security forces to reduce their level of violence to something like an acceptable level.

Yet it summed up with rather too much succinctness British policy. In the memory of the people Maudling is associated with two unpalatable but essentially subjectively true remarks: the 'acceptable level' of violence and his cry on 1 July 1970, shortly after taking over responsibility, to a stewardess on his plane back to London, 'For God's sake bring me a large Scotch. What a bloody awful country!'

On 12 March 1971, 4,000 shipyard workers marched in Belfast demanding the internment of PIRA leaders, and Chichester-Clarke, like all Unionist prime ministers before him, quailed at the sight. He sought a meeting with Maudling to ask for increased security measures and was not granted them. Worn out and with support slipping away from him he resigned on 20 March and later entered the House of Lords as Baron Moyola of Castledawson, his old parliamentary constituency. He was succeeded on 23 March by Faulkner, who easily beat his rival Craig by twenty-six votes to four. He began judiciously enough by offering to the Social Democratic and Labour Party (SDLP) chairmanships of two important committees, the first time nationalists would be involved in the running of Northern Ireland affairs.[2] The acceptance was made impossible when an inquiry into the deaths of two Derry men shot by the army in the Bogside on 8 July was refused by the government and, persuaded by Hume, the party members withdrew from Stormont.

Now Faulkner decided to hold another recruiting drive for the IRA. Obviously he had no such idea but his action in introducing internment without trial had precisely that effect. Loyalist persuasion for the move was strong and vocal, and it had worked beautifully during the IRA 'Border Campaign' of the late 1950s. Maudling was strongly against it; for all his appearance of detachment and casualness he was an astute politician, on the liberal wing of the party, and knew what could easily happen. When his objections were ignored he said to Faulkner, 'Lift some Protestants if you can.' In fact, of the 343 internees who were brutally lifted and badly treated at 4am on 9 August 1971, there were very few Protestants and those who were detained were associated with the civil rights agitation. The arresting soldiers were accompanied by RUC Special Branch officers whose lists were woefully out of date.

In the violent rioting that followed eleven civilians and one soldier were killed in Belfast, among them Fr Hugh Murray who was shot while administering last rites in Ballymurphy, and a UDR soldier on the Tyrone–Donegal border, and barricades reappeared in the Bogside. One hundred and sixteen of those lifted were released in forty-eight hours, one a printer whose only sign of quasi-illegal activity was the production of material for the PDs. Fewer than eighty of those interned in Crumlin Road jail and the *Maidstone*, a converted troopship, were PIRA members and none significant. Those retained were subject to the techniques of modern interrogation: torture, sleep deprivation, white noise, hooding and starvation. There followed months of disaffection among the nationalist community. Rent and rates strikes followed and the toll of death and serious injury rose. The total of those killed in 1971 was 180, half of them civilians. Faulkner's hubristic gamble had failed and the writing on the wall spelled the fall of Stormont. Many young nationalists rushed to join the PIRA, assenting for better or worse to the presence of paramilitaries in their communities.

Internment was to lead to one of the blackest days in the history of the Troubles. On Saturday, 22 January 1972 a protest march walked along Magilligan Strand in north County Derry to protest at the compound of the prison there. It passed off relatively peacefully though the army fired some token rubber bullets. Another anti-internment march was fixed for the following Sunday week, 30 January. A few stones were thrown that day and then, in spite of advice from the local head of the RUC, District Inspector Frank Lagan, the members of the Parachute Regiment and the Green Howards shot twenty-six unarmed people, thirteen of whom died in the streets and a fourteenth later of his wounds; some of the fatalities were minors. A tribunal under the Lord Chief Justice of England, John Widgery (1911–1981), set up soon after the event, to no one's surprise exonerated the army when it reported in April. But Bloody Sunday, as it inevitably came to be called, would not go away. It caused countrywide rage and grief, and led so many young people to flock to join the PIRA that it could hardly cope with the numbers. On the Wednesday following Bloody Sunday, a crowd of 35,000 people converged on the British Embassy in Dublin and burnt it to the ground. After two months of tremendous violence, including the killing of seven people at Aldershot by an Official IRA (OIRA) bomb on 22 February (the victims were five canteen women, a Catholic chaplain and a gardener), the OIRA murder attempt on the life of John Taylor, the Unionist Minister of State, which he survived, and the killing of two women and the injuring of 130 other people by a no-warning PIRA bomb in Belfast's Abercorn Restaurant on 4 March, Stormont fell.

On 24 March Heath announced that since the Faulkner government would not accept the loss of control of law and order the Northern Ireland parliament would be replaced by direct rule from Westminster. The parliament had first met in the Belfast City Hall on 7 June 1921, moved to the palatial Stormont buildings on 16 November 1932, and ceased to exist on a day in March after fifty years and 291 days. Faulkner was its sixth and last prime minister and Unionists could not help feeling that they had suffered a defeat; the jubilation in nationalist areas was hard to bear. That jubilation, however, was somewhat tempered by a power-workers' strike.

Bloody Sunday remains as the most traumatic event of the Troubles in the memory of Derry people. The belief that the army 'ran amok', in the words of the Derry coroner, may not necessarily be true – they may have been following orders – but the full story of that day will not be known for decades. One of the early moves of reconciliation that Tony Blair (1953–) made on the advice of his charismatic Secretary of State for Northern Ireland, Mo Mowlam (1949–2005), when he became prime minister of Britain, was to set up in 1998 the Bloody Sunday tribunal, chaired by Mark Oliver, Baron Saville of Newdigate (1936–). It met in Derry's Guildhall and sat for seven years at a cost in excess of £200 million, eventually making public its findings in 2010. The trauma was intensified because it was believed that the 'Paras' had been brought in to teach the youth of Derry a lesson. The events of 21 July, when eleven people were killed and 130 injured – many critically – by twenty-one PIRA bombs in Belfast, and of 31 August, when the tiny County Derry village of Claudy was devastated by no-warning PIRA bombs and eight people were killed, failed to have the same effect, though the total body count was greater. Bloody Sunday's particular horror consisted in the firing by specially trained soldiers on civilians who were clearly unarmed.

The day's events had a melodramatic postscript in the House of Commons on the Monday following. Maudling's languid attempt at exonerating the army was interrupted by Bernadette Devlin when, after shouting at the Speaker, 'I have a right, as the only representative who was a witness, to ask a question of that murdering hypocrite,' she crossed the chamber, slapped his face and pulled his hair. Afterwards she told reporters, 'I'm sorry I did not go for his throat.'

9

Bloody Attrition

LESSONS HAD, IT SEEMED, BEEN LEARNED at Westminster, if not in Northern Ireland. In March in the black year of 1972 there came a ray of hope at the appointment as Secretary of State for Northern Ireland of William Whitelaw (1918–99), later 1st Viscount Penrith. Known universally as 'Willie' (and soon dubbed 'Willie Whitewash' by the disapproving Paisley), he was genial, tough-minded and brilliant at negotiation. He came within a hair's-breadth of achieving a working peace with the Sunningdale agreement in December 1973. When he was summoned home in November by Edward Heath to help settle the miners' strike it was generally felt that if he had been allowed to stay he might have obviated the Ulster Workers Council's (UWC) strike that brought down the power-sharing executive that was his contribution to the settlement of the Northern Ireland problem.

Whitelaw met members of the PIRA secretly in London during a short-lived truce in early July 1972 and after the carnage of 21 July, called accurately 'Bloody Friday', ordered Operation Motorman which on 31 July ended the so-called 'no-go' areas in Derry and Belfast. The army met with little opposition, though two men were killed in Derry. The intention to remove barricades and allow security force access had been well telegraphed and Republican areas made barely token resistance. Loyalists removed their own obstructions, saying with some unction that they were only established in response to Republican barricades.

The PIRA demands to Whitelaw had been too much for Heath's government. They required an all-Ireland assent to decisions about the North, the withdrawal of the army from 'sensitive areas', and total withdrawal from Irish soil by 1 January 1975. These terms and a general amnesty for all political prisoners, internees, and those on the wanted list proved too much and the Provos determined to continue with the 'armed struggle'. Their demands were impossible to grant in the circumstances. Hopelessly locked in the toils of their own rhetorical traditions they could not understand that more than a million Protestants could not be bombed into a united Ireland, to use a phrase of Cardinal Conway. The background to the continuation of what came to be called the 'long war' is summarised by Marianne Elliott in her book *The Catholics of Ulster* (2000) as follows:

> That [after 'Bloody Sunday'] the IRA went on to become the most ruthless, callous and efficient terrorist movement in modern times should not detract from the early mistakes made by the authorities which helped it on its way... Over the next thirty years two frightened, defensive and resentful working-class communities systematically terrorised each other... By 1993 working-class north Belfast, with some 600 fatalities, had become the blackest spot in Northern Ireland for sectarian murder.

The PIRA always insisted that its enemies were the British army and the RUC. There was no formal sectarian element in their campaign. Yet interpretations of what constituted legitimate targets could be direly flexible. Ancillary workers in police stations were vulnerable, as were shops that supplied goods to the security forces, though even if they didn't they could qualify for attention as 'economic targets'. The most obvious example of what was perceived as doublethink was the killing of members of the almost entirely

Protestant UDR. To the PIRA they were legitimate targets as members of the alien occupying forces, especially since they were believed to contain members of the UVF and of the new paramilitary force, the Ulster Defence Association (UDA), that had been in existence since August 1971 after the violence associated with the imposition of interment. To their families, especially those who lived in west Ulster, they were victims of sectarian murder, causing in time the PIRA to be accused of 'ethnic cleansing', a word borrowed from the new Croatia.

It was part of the PIRA's absolutist mindset that reform was an irrelevance or worse, a distraction from the crusade for a united Ireland with no British connections, after, in the words of Ruairi Ó Brádaigh (1932–) at the Sinn Féin Ard Fheis on 24 October 1971, they had made Northern Ireland 'ungovernable'. The OIRA had already signalled its intention to end abstentionism. Then, on 29 May 1972, after extreme criticism at their killing eight days earlier of a nineteen-year-old Catholic soldier, Ranger William Best, who was home on leave in Derry, the OIRA announced that they were calling a ceasefire because 'The overwhelming desire of all the people of the North is for an end to military action by all sides.' The PIRA and the UDA were unmoved.

The latter numbered 40,000 members by the end of 1972 and began shows of strength with marches in combat uniform and bush hats through Belfast city centre. The authorities made no attempt to stop them. In fact the UDA was a legal organisation until it was proscribed by Sir Patrick Mayhew (1929–), the tenth Secretary of State, on 10 August 1992. They were one of a number of organisations dedicated to the preservation of the Northern Ireland state, which they obstinately called Ulster, in spite of that term's historical inaccuracy. Closely associated with the UDA were the Ulster Freedom Fighters (UFF), perhaps the UDA's cover for some of its blacker deeds. The UDA eventually devised a political wing known as the Ulster Democratic Party (UDP). The UVF had a similar alternative cover name as the Protestant Action Force. A group known as the Red Hand Commando were also associated with the UVF.

The PIRA were similarly not the only active force on the Nationalist side. In 1974 some members of the OIRA, who had disagreed with the ceasefire, formed the Irish National Liberation Army (INLA). It had left-wing tendencies and developed a reputation for greater ruthlessness than the PIRA. Their killing on 30 March 1979 of Airey Neave (1916–79), the close associate of the new prime minister, Margaret – later Baroness – Thatcher (1925–), and her spokesman on Northern Ireland, by a car bomb as he drove out of the car park of the House of Commons, got them world attention. On 6 December 1982 their no-warning bomb at a pub-disco in Ballykelly, County Derry, called the Droppin' Well, killed seventeen people – eleven soldiers from the nearby British base at Walworth camp and six civilians from the village. The INLA insisted that their blanket warning against serving members of the 'occupying forces' was sufficient but the incident was generally condemned. Their associated political party was known as the Irish Republican Socialist Party (IRSP) and gave rise to one of several jokes that even the Troubles could not still. One of the IRSP strongholds was the Lower Falls in Belfast and the Divis Street tower blocks there became known as the 'Planet of the Irps', wordplay on the title of the 1968 film *The Planet of the Apes*.

Each side vied with the other in killings and explosions with little relief from the deadly stasis. Often the attacks were retaliatory or in response to particular occasions, as during the UWC strike in May 1974 and the H-Block hunger strike deaths. The PIRA's enemies were ostensibly the security forces but many civilians died too. The mindless prate that there were no innocent people in the circumstances may have given some comfort to the perpetrators if not to their victims. The slaughter in Claudy was replicated in Enniskillen when a bomb placed close to the war memorial on

Remembrance Sunday, 8 November 1987, intended for – the PIRA said – and detonated by the security forces killed six men and five women, and injured sixty-three others, including children. The father of one of the victims, Gordon Wilson (1927–95), was buried under the rubble near his twenty-year-old daughter Marie. He was able to hold her hand until she died. Wilson, a retired draper, eschewed bitterness and became an active worker for peace. He was later appointed to Seanad Éireann by Taoiseach Albert Reynolds, another activist in the peace process.

Six years later, on the Lower Shankill on 23 October 1993, a no-warning bomb in Frizell's fish shop killed nine people (one died later), including Thomas Begley, one of the bombers, and injured fifty-eight others. Coming as it did when hopes of a PIRA ceasefire were high because of the Hume-Adams peace talks it caused widespread revulsion and inevitable accusations of hypocrisy.

One last IRA atrocity should be mentioned: on 15 August 1998, four months after the Good Friday Agreement, the Real IRA, a dissident group that did not accept the terms of the agreement, exploded a 500lb bomb in Lower Main Street, Omagh. It killed nineteen adults and nine children (a twenty-ninth victim died on 5 September). Though the Real IRA, accepting responsibility, said that all military operations were being suspended it was believed that some of its members joined the Continuity IRA, the only Republican paramilitary group not on ceasefire. They *do* continue the same pattern of threats, arson of large stores, and have retained the exaltation of the 'armed struggle'.

Loyalist paramilitaries were not idle, with random killing of Catholics and bombing of Catholic businesses. As with Republican groups the campaign to save Ulster and prevent a united Ireland was kept to a general, almost quotidian, level of violence with occasional spectacular atrocities. The killing of fifteen people by the UVF in McGurk's bar in Belfast on 4 December 1971 marked the culmination of a bleak year. Other actions by loyalists include the explosions on 17 May 1974 in Monaghan and Dublin that killed a total of eventually thirty people. The UVF and UDA denied responsibility but it is now believed that there was collusion with British 'spooks'.

The total number of fatalities in 1975 was 247, of which 217 were civilians. Some of the incidents were particularly chilling, arising mainly out of 'tit-for-tat' killings. On Saturday, 5 April a bomb thrown into McLaughlin's bar in north Belfast killed two Catholics; it was answered by a bomb three hours later in a Shankill Road pub that killed five Protestants. On 31 July three members of the Miami Showband were shot dead when their van was flagged down near Newry by the UVF. They lost two of their own number when a bomb intended to blow up the van went off prematurely. On 5 January 1976 a bus carrying Protestant workers was stopped at Kingsmill, County Armagh. The ten workers were machine-gunned; the Catholic driver escaped. The 'Kingsmill massacre' was in retaliation for the killing the previous day of five Catholics at Whitecross in the same county. The Shankill bombings of October 1993 were the claimed cause of the notorious 'Trick-or-Treat' shootings in Greysteel, County Derry one week later on 30 October. UFF gunmen killed seven people in the Rising Sun bar there, one taking time to reload. The dead included two women and an eighty-one-year-old man. One of the dead was a local Protestant.

The killing continued, extended by the PIRA to England. The 'Birmingham Six' case involved six men sentenced to life for their alleged responsibility for the bombing of two pubs in Birmingham on 21 November 1974 in which twenty-one people died. They were freed in 1991 after seventeen years in prison after the longest campaign against a miscarriage of justice in legal history. The main campaigners were Chris Mullins, a Labour MP, Peter Barry, the Irish Foreign Minister, Fr Denis Faul and Fr Raymond Murray of the Armagh archdiocese, and Bishop Edward Daly of Derry, who had become famous as the priest with the white handkerchief as he ministered to the dying on Bloody Sunday. The release of the 'Guildford Four', who had also been sentenced to life for the pub bombs in Guildford and Woolwich on 5 October and 7 November 1974 on the basis of confessions later retracted, gave greater impetus to the Birmingham Six agitation. Though the PIRA gained little but condemnation for their English campaign the reputation of the British legal system sank, giving rise to such cracks as 'It's a principle of British justice that you're innocent until proved Irish' and 'Britain waives the rules.'

In spite of the adverse affect on the Irish of the diaspora, settled in Britain, that the bombing campaign inevitably had, the PIRA continued to believe that it was a useful and, of course, legitimate part of its campaign. One of their more notorious 'spectaculars' – as these special events were called – was the attempt to kill Margaret Thatcher, then prime minister, and her cabinet at 2.54am on 12 October 1984 in the Grand Hotel, Brighton, during the Conservative annual conference. Six people were killed but the only member of the cabinet to be injured was Norman – later Baron – Tebbit of Chingford. The PIRA were reported as having commented at the time, 'We only have to be lucky once.' The return of a fourth Conservative government on Friday, 10 April 1992 was commented upon by the PIRA with a 100lb Semtex bomb at the Baltic Exchange in the City of London that killed three people, injured ninety-one, and caused £700 million worth of damage; and the 1994 PIRA ceasefire was ended abruptly at 7.01pm on 9 February 1996, with a bomb at Canary Wharf which killed two people, injured more than a hundred, and did more than £85 million damage, slowing the peace process and causing Sinn Féin to express surprise. The relentless need for decommissioning that the Democratic Unionist Party (DUP), founded in 1971 by Ian Paisley, and soon to become the largest Unionist party, demanded dates from that event.

Back in Northern Ireland most town centres were bombed, some several times. Security gates became a feature of urban life as also were often unpleasant body searches. Army and police checkpoints were imposed without warning and a city like Derry, its two parts joined until 1984 by a single bridge, with its main hospitals and railway station on the east bank and its fire station on the west, suffered greatly and often dangerously from traffic disruption.

During the Second World War a psychosomatic phenomenon known as 'war weariness' began to affect the civilian population. Psychologists looked for the same syndrome in Northern Ireland but failing to find any notable evidence of it concluded that a combination of native stoicism and high adrenalin had kept it at bay because of the localised nature of the conflict. They did, however, warn of some dysfunctional response if peace should return.

The 'war' consisted largely of localised violence, if one excluded the dangers of 'economic targets', being confined largely to working class nationalist areas, where even young children regarded the BA, as the army was known, and the RUC as sworn enemies. They also were enmeshed in mutual fear with Protestants of sectarian violence. Middle class people throughout Northern Ireland had less to fear but dreaded the possible involvement of their children, especially at times of heightened emotions, such as the UWC strike of 1974 and the hunger strike deaths of 1981. The slightly illogical belief that their own areas were safe as opposed to other areas tended to discourage unnecessary travel though journeys across the border to the political South tended among nationalists to increase.

10

Looking for an Answer

FROM THE BEGINNING OF DIRECT RULE in March 1972 until the end of the 1990s there were in all twelve Secretaries of State for Northern Ireland, four from the Labour Party: Merlyn Rees (1974–6), Roy Mason (1976–9), Mo Mowlam (1997–9), and Peter Mandelson (1999–2001); and eight Conservatives: William Whitelaw (1972–3), Francis Pym (1973–4), Humphrey Atkins (1979–81), James Prior (1981–4), Douglas Hurd (1984–5), Tom King (1985–9), Sir Peter Brooke (1989–92) and Sir Patrick Mayhew (1992–7). They varied greatly in approach and talent but each (with the exception of Mason) tried to set up some system of government that would allow a workable devolution. Whitelaw almost succeeded with the powersharing executive generated by the Sunningdale Agreement. He was summoned, as we have seen, by Heath, rattled by the miners' strike at home, and was not able to complete his work. His successor, Pym, did what he could during his short stay but after the general election of February 1974 that the Conservatives lost he was replaced by Merlyn Rees who was faced with the humiliation of the UWC strike of May of that year. Whitelaw's work almost succeeded. With Faulkner as Chief Executive and Gerry Fitt as deputy it began well. John Hume's increasingly important position was recognised by his being made Minister of Finance.

It split Unionism. Paisley, Harry West (1917–2004), who had ousted Faulkner as leader of the Ulster Unionist Party (UUP), and William Craig joined an organising committee led by Glenn Barr (1932–) of the Vanguard Party, established by Craig in 1973. It was hard for them to stomach the idea of even the mild SDLP having power in government when it was a deep-rooted belief that the only people who should be in government were the Unionists. The stoppage succeeded in its purpose because the power workers supported it and Protestant paramilitaries used intimidation where necessary. The army made no attempt to dismantle roadblocks and with little direction from Rees did not quite know how to proceed. The intermittent power-cuts meant that filling stations could not supply petrol, though a few resurrected manual systems of delivery. As ever Belfast was the most sorely affected. In border areas it became customary to cross into Donegal, Monaghan and Louth to fill up. Many who boasted that they never entered 'Éire' managed to overcome their reluctance. Since the stoppage took place in late spring most people were able to withstand the lack of power for heating but it was the threat that the sewage systems might back up that caused the greatest worry. The most serious violence occurred not in Northern Ireland but, as we have seen, in Monaghan and Dublin. The Unionists in the Executive finally resigned on 28 May and the strike and the powersharing were over.

Nationalists were greatly disappointed and dismayed. They had seen the RUC chatting happily with UDA members carrying clubs at illegal barricades and accused Rees of inertia. He, with typical phlegm, announced his attempt at solution in 1975, a 'constitutional convention' to find a system 'likely to command the most widespread acceptance' but since the Unionists were elected to forty-seven of the total seventy-eight seats, and would consider only the terms of the original 1920 Act, it came to nothing. A similar initiative by James Prior (1927–) in 1982 that became known as 'rolling devolution' achieved little and was discontinued by Prior's successor Douglas Hurd. Rees was followed by Roy Mason (1924–) under whose regime the idea of a military defeat of the IRA was advanced. This was more an expression of his own rather abrasive personality than of any actual belief in the policy. Rees had warned the cabinet just before he left office that British government involvement in Northern Ireland's affairs was 'for the long haul'.

As the state papers for 1976 show, Harold Wilson (1916–95), just before his retirement as prime minister in the autumn, was so despairing of the situation that he was considering pulling out and leaving the North to settle its own affairs as best it might. Since this would have meant the nationalist majority being direly vulnerable in the face of Protestant paramilitaries, and an uneven civil war would have resulted, the Dublin government were greatly relieved when Callaghan indicated that his government would stay to see things out. This was reiterated on 12 September 1977 by Mason when he announced that the 'myth of British withdrawal' was 'now dead for ever'.

With the PIRA's assassination by landmine of the British ambassador, Christopher Ewart-Biggs (1921–76), on 21 July 1976, a fortnight after his appointment, relations between London and Dublin seemed to have reached rock bottom but the declaration of a state of emergency in the South and a series of additional anti-terrorism measures began again a slow but effective healing which continued to strengthen during the following three decades until 'the Irish dimension' had become a vital part of any possible solution.

Mason's tough policy seemed to have produced some diminution in the level of violence. He successfully broke another attempt by Paisley to have a rerun of the UWC strike in May 1977. The army were directed to disperse Loyalist roadblocks as soon as they were set up and he was crucially aided by the fact that the power workers did not support the stoppage. Though the end of the 'special category' imprisonment allowed by Whitelaw, that treated prisoners rather like POWs kept in compounds with a command structure, occurred at the end of Rees's term of office it was Mason that implemented it with gusto.

'Criminalisation' meant that prisoners could no longer wear their own clothes or have the privileges granted by Whitelaw. They were housed in the new Maze prison near Lisburn, County Antrim, that had blocked buildings in the shape of the letter H. Protests began almost immediately: prisoners draped themselves in blankets and began the 'dirty protest' that meant no use of toilet facilities. Their cells, which they refused to leave, were often smeared with excrement. Cardinal Tomás Ó Fiaich (1923–90), Cardinal Conway's successor, led the worldwide protest about conditions, having visited the H-Blocks and found the milieu indescribable. Mason would not yield, preferring to advance the cause of the 'Peace People', Mairéad Corrigan, Betty Williams and Ciaran McKeown.

Corrigan was the aunt of three children who had been killed in the Belfast area of Andersonstown by a gunman's getaway car when he was shot by the army. The two women organised a series of impromptu 'peace' marches that received much support. Financial backing came from Norway, Germany and America and they were recipients of the 1976 Nobel Peace Prize. The phenomenon lasted until the end of the 1970s, causing initially consternation in the ranks of the paramilitaries. Without a specific platform it could not last but its spontaneous popularity and the thousands who attended the peace rallies throughout Ireland and abroad showed with what eagerness its goal was wished for.

One other event of Mason's tenure was the £56 million subsidy for John De Lorean and his futurist car with wing doors and stainless steel chassis. The project collapsed but the car, now a collector's item, may be seen each Christmas when the film *Back to the Future* (1985), which includes a De Lorean car as one of its stars, is broadcast on television.

Mason was replaced by Humphrey Atkins (1922–96) when the

Conservatives under Margaret Thatcher were returned to power in May 1979. His appointment to the post Airey Neave had been intended for was something of a surprise. The PIRA celebrated the new regime with two same-day spectaculars on 27 August. Lord Mountbatten of Burma (1900–79), his fourteen-year-old grandson, and a boy crew member were killed instantly and the Dowager Lady Brabourne died later from her injuries when Mountbatten's boat was blown to pieces by a radio-controlled bomb at Mullaghmore in County Sligo, near his house at Classiebawn; and eighteen soldiers died in a bomb attack at Narrow Water Castle in Warrenpoint, County Down. Thatcher visited the North two days later and promised 1,000 new men for the RUC. Pope John Paul II, who was about to begin his Irish tour, decided against visiting Armagh but, coming as far north as was feasible, in Drogheda on 29 September, appealed 'on bended knees' for an end to violence. The PIRA rejected the pope's appeal on 2 October saying that they had wide support and that only the armed struggle would remove the British. Thatcher, already demonstrating the right-wing inflexibility that led to her being called the 'Iron Lady', was determined to increase security, having no obvious desire to find a political solution.

Atkins went through the usual steps of the complicated dance measure, usually a saraband, required by Northern secretaries. His initiative was a Constitutional Conference held in Stormont, from January to March in 1980. The DUP refused to attend and so too did the SDLP initially, causing Gerry Fitt to resign. Atkins' term of office produced one of the greatest crises in the whole of the current troubles. The one traditional weapon that the PIRA prisoners had not yet used officially in their struggle against 'criminalisation' was the hunger strike. Seven prisoners, dismayed at the lack of success of the 'blanket' and 'dirty' protests, began a strike on 27 October 1980. It lasted until 18 December when Atkins seemed to have offered some concessions of clothing. The offer was not what the prisoners took it to be and Bobby Sands (1954–1981), OC of the

H-Blocks, began another strike 'to the death' on 1 March 1981. He was to be joined by another striker each week. His election in Fermanagh–South Tyrone three weeks before his death, defeating Harry West, the former leader of the Unionist Party, by 1,446 votes, gave a great boost to the campaign. His funeral on 7 May was attended by 70,000 mourners and, as was to be the case with the funerals of other strikers, there was serious rioting in Belfast and Derry.

All during the summer of 1981 deaths in the H-Blocks blighted life in the North. The sequential nature of the protest meant that, in spite of protests and recommendations by Dublin to other governments to intervene, the ghastly regularity continued. The second man to die was Francis Hughes who survived sixty-one days, dying on 12 May. He was followed by Patsy O'Hara, leader of the INLA prisoners, and Raymond McCreesh on 21 May. Joe McDonnell died on 8 July, Martin Hurson on 13 July, Kevin Lynch on 1 August, Kieran Doherty, who had been elected TD in June, the next day, Thomas McElwee on 8 August, and Michael Devine on 20 August. Garret FitzGerald (1926–2011), who had been elected Taoiseach on 30 June, Charles Haughey (1925–2005), the previous Taoiseach, Cardinal Ó Fiaich, and John Hume tried to apply pressure on the British government but the Iron Lady lived up to her sobriquet. One of those who had campaigned vigorously for prisoners' rights and documented evidence about army and police brutality was Fr Denis Faul (1932–2006), a priest of the Armagh diocese, who had acted as prison chaplain. He strongly disapproved of the strike and managed to encourage the families of the remaining strikers to persuade them to end their action. The PIRA described him as a 'treacherous, conniving man' but they called off the strike on 3 October. The campaign had led to the deaths of sixty-one people, including thirty members of the security forces. Three days later James Prior, the new Secretary of State, announced that prisoners could now wear their own clothing.

Though Thatcher's hard line on the strikes seemed to have prevailed there was no decrease in violence. The long-drawn-out sequence of slow dying, death, emotional funerals and concomitant rioting made it the most depressing time of the Troubles. Yet for a number of reasons it marked a turning point in the process. Catholics and Protestants became even more polarised. Though many nationalists believed that the calling of the strike was a form of blackmail they responded to the painful sacrifices made by the strikers. Unionists were shocked that so many had voted for Bobby Sands and they were appalled at the numbers that attended the funerals. The rise of Sinn Féin, as the political wing of the PIRA, began then, as did a persistent involvement of the various Dublin governments. The 'Irish dimension' of the mid-1970s now grew to participation in Anglo-Irish agreements. This political activity was regularly punctuated by bombing and shooting but a change was beginning to be felt. Danny Morrison (1940–), Sinn Féin's publicity director in the 1981 elections, coined the slick phrase 'with a ballot box in one hand and an Armalite in the other' as their means of achieving power. It annoyed many people but it conveyed succinctly the PIRA's intention.

One effect of their entry into politics was the erosion of the Fianna Fáil vote, enabling Fine Gael under the leadership of Garret FitzGerald to coalesce with Labour and form a short-lived administration in June 1981. Haughey, who had been Taoiseach, blamed Thatcher for his defeat and his relations with her afterwards were cool. FitzGerald called himself the 'revolving-door Taoiseach' because his government's stringent budget proposals caused him to lose office the following February but his meetings with Thatcher established the Anglo-Irish Intergovernmental Council on 6 November 1981. Paisley branded Thatcher 'a traitor and a liar' four days later and tried to set up a 'Third Force', a vigilante band to settle security, a kind of B-specials regenerated. Their public appearances, apart from some very intimidating UDA-manned roadblocks, were rather like those of the followers of the 'grand old Duke of York'. FitzGerald returned to power on 24 November 1982 and, finding compatible ideological affinity with the Labour leader Dick Spring (1950–), managed to sustain the coalition until January 1987. His chief contribution to the amelioration of Northern affairs was his devising of the New Ireland Forum (NIF). This was a conference, prompted by Hume, of the four main constitutional nationalist parties Fianna Fáil, Fine Gael, Labour and SDLP. Sinn Féin was excluded because of its support for violence, and the Unionists unsurprisingly boycotted it. It was the first stepping stone on the yellow brick road to the Downing Street Declaration of 15 December 1993 made by the British Prime Minister John Major (1943–) and Taoiseach Albert Reynolds (1932–).

The Forum report was published on 3 May 1984 and made three alternative proposals. The first was for a unitary thirty-two county state, which was unlikely in the current situation, the second was for some kind of federal arrangement, and the third indicated a joint authority in Northern Ireland by the British and Irish governments. These propositions were rejected by Thatcher on 19 November 1984 in her speech since known as 'Out! Out! Out!' What she did actually say was:

> I have made it quite clear, and so did Mr Prior when he was Secretary of State for Northern Ireland, that a unified Ireland was one solution. That is out. A second solution was confederation of the two states. That is out. A third solution was joint authority. That is out. That is derogation from sovereignty.

Even the imperturbable FitzGerald blinked once or twice at such a public rejection. It was only five weeks after the Brighton bombing and she could not in the circumstances show anything that might give succour to the IRA. Her tendency towards dramatic sound bites merely hid a clever politician who realised that negotiation was the only way forward. Discussions began almost immediately and they culminated in the Anglo-Irish Agreement (AIA) of 1985.

The agreement was signed at Hillsborough on 15 November to Unionist fury. The significant parts of the AIA were summarised in Articles One and Two:

> The two governments… affirm that any change in the status of Northern Ireland would come about only with the consent of a majority of the people of Northern Ireland…
>
> The United Kingdom Government accept that the Irish Government will put forward views and proposals on matters relating to Northern Ireland… in so far as these matters are not the responsibility of a devolved administration in Northern Ireland. In the interests of peace and stability, determined efforts shall be made through the conference to resolve any differences.

An Anglo-Irish Intergovernmental Conference was set up and chaired by the Irish Minister for Foreign Affairs and the Northern Secretary. The headquarters was at Maryfield, near Holywood in County Down, and was staffed twenty-four hours a day by British and Irish civil servants.

The AIA was a giant step on the road to a solution, something better than Churchill's wartime phrase, 'the end of the beginning'. Nine weary years would elapse before the necessary ceasefires but the light descried at the end of the tunnel was at least not that of an oncoming train. Unionists reacted negatively as they regarded any change as favouring the nationalist cause and eroding their position. They dreamed of a restoration of the old Stormont system and were reluctant to accept the fact that it was merely a dream. Posters and banners appeared in all possible – if not always appropriate – places asserting, 'Ulster Says "No!"'. One prominent one draped on the classical pediment at the front of the City Hall in Belfast was emended with unexpected pleasantry at Christmas to read, 'Belfast Says "Noel."'

The Downing Street Declaration, eight years later, was the product of much joint work between the governments and could not have taken place without the preliminary talks between John Hume and Gerry Adams (1948–) who had become president of Sinn Féin in 1983. Adams was a Falls Road Catholic, interned in 1971 but released in 1972 to take part in the talks with Whitelaw that led to a brief ceasefire. He was one of the leading thinkers in Sinn Féin and the man most prominent in persuading the PIRA to become a participant political party. His talks with Hume led to accusations from Unionists that nationalists had formed a pan-nationalist front but critics of Sinn Féin on both sides were beginning to be persuaded that the PIRA could not be defeated militarily. Peter Brooke, the ninth Northern Secretary since the fall of Stormont, admitted as much in a speech in 1990, saying in his polite way that 'it is difficult to envisage a military defeat of the IRA'. It was this quasi-aristocratic politeness, which concealed a very astute political brain, that ended his seemingly self-effacing career as a politician when he could not resist an invitation by Gay Byrne to sing on the *Late Late Show* of 17 January 1992 on RTÉ, eight hours after the killing of eight Protestant workers engaged in a contract for the security forces at Omagh at Teebane Cross by a 1,500lb PIRA bomb. Brooke had hoped to meet Adams and, with hindsight, seems one of the more agreeable and liberal of all the secretaries. Incidentally, he was not a good singer.

Adams needed to persuade his people that just as they could not be defeated, equally they could not win. The seizure on 31 October 1987 by the French of an old ship, the *Eksund*, with an Irish crew, containing 150 tonnes of armaments, including guns and the new Czech explosive Semtex, made it clear that Colonel Gadaffi of Libya was the PIRA's chief supplier. When it was further established that this was the fourth such cargo it was obvious that the PIRA had enough material to carry on war without end. The old dream of driving out the British by force and of thereby establishing a united Republican Ireland provided enough exaltation for hardliners to continue. They had received a setback on 8 May with the miscarrying of a carefully planned operation against the RUC station in Loughgall, County Armagh. Eight prominent PIRA activists were shot by SAS soldiers who were now involved in 'counter-terrorism' and had prior warning of the attack. The guns recovered had been used lethally thirty-three times in other operations.

The Loughgall attack gave rise to severe rioting in Belfast and Derry. The notorious Enniskillen Remembrance Day bombing followed on 8 November. After the killing of eight young British soldiers on 20 August, Adams had much work to do, hampered by Thatcher's injunction that he be denied the 'oxygen of publicity'. Hurd, who had served as Northern Ireland Secretary in 1984–5, as Home Secretary now brought in stringent censorship rules about the content and vocalisation of Sinn Féin statements. Actors' voices were dubbed over the media statements of Adams and his associate Martin McGuinness (1950–), once head of the PIRA in Derry, and who became chief negotiator in the many talks that were to take place for nearly a score more years. The results of the vocal censorship were risible and self-defeating, pleasing no one but the actors' union, Equity, and the rules were not relaxed until after the 1994 ceasefire.

The death toll due to the Troubles for the 1980s totalled 792. It was less than half of the total for the 1970s at 1,991 but still meant appalling and unnecessary suffering. The majority population of Northern Ireland were caught between two forms of intransigence: the British government's refusal to treat with 'terrorists' while they carried on their relentless armed struggle and that of the various republican groups, certain that nothing else would achieve their objectives. A third element in the situation was the murderous activity of loyalist paramilitaries, usually sectarian, but occasionally directed against the security forces. In spite of this, attempts at some kind of normal life continued. Outside of working class areas of the larger towns and other parts of the North where particular types of politics flourished it was possible to ignore the military presence, though open-topped Land Rovers manned by heavily-armed soldiers with pointing guns, and mixed patrols of RUC and military personnel who could establish checkpoints in minutes, were not so easy to turn a blind eye to. The recurring cry and gable-end insistence that Ulster was British was rejected by almost all of the nationalist population who in turn found a greater identification with the South, if not politically since they had no general concern with the minutiae of its internal problems, then culturally. *Gaelscoileanna*, where children were taught through the medium of Irish, began to be established with no explicit political agenda, and Irish drama flourished.

One of the more interesting cultural phenomena of the 1980s was the Field Day theatrical company founded by Brian Friel (1929–) and the actor Stephen Rea (1952–) in 1980 and including on its board Seamus Deane (1940–), David Hammond, Seamus Heaney (1939–) and Tom Paulin (1949–). Its purpose was to redefine Ireland's cultural identity through drama, pamphlets, and the three-volume Field Day *Anthology of Irish Writing* (1991). The plays written by Friel, Derek Mahon, Paulin, Heaney, Thomas Kilroy, Stewart Parker and others gave Derry, the scene of the first productions, a dozen years of political drama and theatrical fame. The period saw also the flowering of the work of such Irish poets as Heaney (who won the Nobel Prize for Literature in 1995), Michael Longley (1939–), and Derek Mahon (1941–). Their approach to the Troubles was appropriately delayed and oblique but in such poems as Heaney's 'Casualty' and Longley's 'The Ice-Cream Man' contain the essence of the time.

The Troubles were not able to stifle theatre. Mary O'Malley's Lyric continued to operate even during the UWC strike. One of its successes sprang straight from the Northern Ireland situation. This was *The Flats* by John Boyd who also helped to edit the journal *Threshold*, associated with the Lyric. Other theatrical enterprises included Charabanc, Big Telly, Tinderbox, and DubbelJoint. The last of these featured work by Marie Jones of Charabanc. To indicate its commitment to audiences throughout the whole island of Ireland its title came from the jointure of the 'Dub' of Dublin and the 'Bel' of Belfast.

11

Peace-by-Piece Process?

IN HIS BRILLIANTLY WITTY AND SATIRICAL attack on nineteenth-century values, *Eminent Victorians* (1918), Lytton Strachey (1880–1932), the Bloomsbury essayist and biographer, wrote: 'Ignorance is the first requisite of the historian – ignorance, which simplifies and clarifies, which selects and omits, with a placid perfection unattainable by the highest art.'

Contemplating the complexity of the Northern Ireland Troubles one could wish perversely with equivalent Stracheyean tongue-in-cheek for some such shapely lack of knowledge. The Northern Ireland situation has generated such a prodigious amount of verbal and written comment that one longs for simplification and clarification. Over the years so many initiatives have been originated only to falter because of the reasons stated earlier. Most of the books written have dealt with the violence and the political aspects of the situation. Less has been chronicled of many attempts at economic improvements in the North. In the early days of the Troubles the tourist trade in both parts of Ireland suffered severely though a certain curiosity about the embattled North brought visitors to the safer South from which they made conscience-salving brief incursions into Ulster and even Northern Ireland. This situation gradually improved during the 1990s and Southern Ireland started to benefit from an economic surge that began during the decade. This occurred because of its openness to investment from multinationals and the quality of its young, ambitious and highly educated workforce. Many parts of Ireland claimed never to have experienced even the roar of the Celtic Tiger, as it came to be known, but in general, unfavourable comparisons economically with the North, almost entirely financed by the British taxpayer, no longer held. The realisation of the advantages of cross-border economics began to exercise the Northern Irish Office (NIO), the centre of government since the abolition of Stormont.

From the point of view of outside investors the troubled North was not obviously attractive. In vain the Westminster government and the NIO tried to persuade American and Asian companies that the attractiveness of the South as an appropriate location of investment was replicated in the North. Apart from a few disturbed areas, they argued, the same ideal conditions existed. The continued selection of economic targets by the PIRA did not help their argument. The bombing of the Baltic Exchange in April 1992 was a classical example of an economic 'spectacular'. The Downing Street bomb on 12 October was a more specifically political caper. 'Mainland' attacks (the word not accepted by nationalists) were often less specific.

On Saturday, 20 March 1993 'shopping' bombs in litter bins in Warrington killed among others two young boys aged three and twelve, and caused such a wave of disgust in both Ireland and Britain that it is believed that PIRA chiefs warned local activists against attacks that would prove politically disadvantageous. The general revulsion felt was similar to that generated by the first 'proxy' bomb in which Patsy Gillespie, who the PIRA said worked for the security forces, was strapped into a van loaded with explosives and forced, on 24 October 1990, to drive into the Coshquin permanent checkpoint near the Donegal border on the Derry–Buncrana Road, killing himself and five soldiers. Even as late as 15 June 1996 a 'mainland' target proved irresistible: a bomb wiped out much of the city centre of Manchester injuring 250 people, allowing it to share the fate of every town in Northern Ireland.

None of this contributed much to the search for economic investment in the North. By now, however, John Hume had attained international status. His fluency in French proved useful with the European parliament but it was in the United States that his talent for persuasion was used most successfully. He managed to secure American investment for his native city and surrounding districts, a region notably starved of enterprise under the old regime. He was on friendly terms with Senator Ted Kennedy (1932–2009), John F Kennedy's youngest brother, and the influential 'Tip' O'Neill (1912–94), Speaker of the House of Representatives, and soon was able to direct and intensify the concern for Irish matters already shown by the new president, Bill Clinton (1946–), elected in 1994.

Peter Brooke was replaced by Sir Patrick Mayhew (1929–) who was the tenth Secretary of State and served longest, ceasing only when a change of government in 1997 brought Mo Mowlam. Mayhew had been attorney-general and unlike each previous secretary did not regard his appointment as a form of exile. Up till then Northern Ireland had been regarded as the graveyard of political ambitions. Mayhew had been keen to accept and with a legal/army background felt he might have something to contribute. Like Brooke he was suave, talented, courteous, and had a skein of Anglo-Irishness in his make-up, but this did not impress the Dublin government. Michael Mates (1934–), his second-in-command, was rather more abrasive and had an army background also, actually having served in the North with the rank of Lieutenant-Colonel.

Contacts with Sinn Féin had by now been such an ingrained part of the security system that Mayhew could not have discontinued them, even if he had wanted to. His proscription of the UDA on 10 August 1992, one his earliest acts as Northern Secretary, pleased nationalists. It had been allowed to appear legal for far too long despite being responsible for many sectarian murders and its banning, though scandalously overdue, allowed Mayhew to appear to be as stern with the PIRA and the INLA. He was consulted about the Downing Street Declaration and worked well with David Andrews (1935–), the Irish Minister for Foreign Affairs. The early years of his office were marked by a kind of bipolarity on the part of Republicans. Talks ostensibly secret continued in the midst of murderous violence. Perhaps it is fanciful to suggest that Sinn Féin's weaning of PIRA from the armed struggle was rather like the treatment of alcoholism or drug addiction. There was no possibility of cold turkey and the cessation required some ideological methadone that would ease the crossover. Or perhaps another metaphor might come from a family structure by which the parents must wait till the wildest of the children are ready to make the change, urging with full parental authority that change must be made.

The Downing Street Declaration indicated a tremendous leap forward on the part of the two governments and both John Major and Albert Reynolds must be seen as significant peacemakers. Their joint statement comprised five principles that finally reconciled Republicans to the idea of talks that would lead to a ceasefire, and convinced constitutional nationalists that things were moving in the right direction. Unionists needed more persuasion, believing that anything that pleased 'pan-nationalism' must naturally be to their disadvantage, though it did contain significant guarantees. It stated first that the people of Ireland, North and South, should be free to determine their own future. This had appended the pious hope that that future 'should ideally lead to the possibility, ultimately of unity on this island'. The second concerned 'the development of new structures for the government of Northern Ireland and for relationships between North and South and with Britain'. Thirdly no such agreements could be reached without the consent of a majority in the North. The fourth strand gave Unionists the right to withhold their consent and the fifth imposed on the Dublin government the duty of consenting to any democratic agreement once achieved. Lastly the 'men of violence' must be accepted as participants in negotiation once they had eschewed that violence.

It was a carefully worded, diplomatically crafted document that had enough ambivalences to reassure the suspicious. Adams required 'clarification', which was correctly seen as a willingness to parlay, and Major, dependant on Unionist MPs to boost his shaky majority, emphasised for their benefit in his speech in the House of Commons what was not in the declaration. In spite of hesitations, repetitions and deviations, and agonisingly slow progress, the active search for solution known as the 'Peace Process' began its lumbering advance.

In spite of uneasy governmental tenure both in Westminster and Dublin but with pressure from Clinton, and continuing talking between Hume and Adams, the PIRA declared a permanent ceasefire on 31 August 1994. Six weeks later, on 13 October, the loyalist paramilitaries, including the UDA, UVF and the Red Hand Commando, using the umbrella term 'Combined Loyalist Military Command', announced a ceasefire, having consulted with loyalist prisoners in the Maze prison three days earlier. There was a remarkable atmospheric change in Northern Ireland. Soldiers wore berets instead of helmets on patrol and in Belfast the RUC were unaccompanied by the military and had shed their flak jackets. Town centres became alive again, most notably in Belfast. This post-bellum euphoria continued even after Gerry Adams's remark at a rally in Belfast on 13 August 1995 about the PIRA, 'They haven't gone away, you know!', finding it necessary to remind his listeners that affairs though moving in the right direction had some distance yet to travel.

Even as he was speaking preparations had begun for another 'spectacular' in London. The PIRA, frustrated by slow progress and having to keep its extreme members content, planned an attack for the following spring. John Bruton (1947–), leader of Fine Gael, who became Taoiseach on 15 December 1994, had a different approach to Reynolds. He was less patient with the formal dance of the Peace Process, now always printed with upper-case initials, and had frequently harsh things to say about the PIRA's 'weasel words'. He continued with the Forum for Peace and Reconciliation that Reynolds had established on 28 October and, on 22 February, launched jointly with Major a *Framework for the Future* document indicating the fine details of a possible settlement. He was distrusted by the Republican movement and seemed like Major to be more interested in pleasing the Unionists than in trying to empathise with the PIRA. American concern and involvement became crucial. Clinton had appointed Jean Kennedy Smith (John F Kennedy's sister) as Irish ambassador on the deliberately chosen date of 17 March 1993 and a special envoy, Senator George Mitchell (1933–), in 1994. Mitchell was to play an important role in easing the vexed question of arms decommissioning and formulating the Belfast Agreement.

On the evening of 9 February 1996 at 7.01pm the PIRA detonated a 1,000lb bomb at Canary Wharf, killing two people, injuring more than 100, and causing damage of more than £85 million. A few minutes earlier they had announced the end of their ceasefire which had lasted seventeen months. There was anger and extreme disappointment; the security forces donned battle gear again. Yet in spite of this bloody setback the search for peace continued. Major's Commons majority was reduced to one on 11 April when Labour won the Staffordshire South East by-election and it was felt that nothing could be done publicly for peace until May 1997, when a general election would surely result in a Labour government. The election, on 2 May, gave Labour a majority of 179 seats so that there was no need to favour Unionists in parliament in return for votes.

Tony Blair, the new Prime Minister, was anxious to re-establish a ceasefire and work towards a devolved government for Northern

Ireland that would be acceptable to all sides. His appointment of Mo Mowlam, a talented and vigorous politician in spite of having to fight cancer, as Secretary, was regarded by nationalists as a great leap forward. By July she had her first great test in the business of the violence generated by the yearly stand-off at Drumcree, the Anglican church on a hill overlooking the contentious town of Portadown.

The 1980s and 1990s had seen an increase of polarisation, both psychologically and even geographically. In the past Northern Ireland had known a certain amount of functional amity but as the Troubles continued both sides retreated into self-imposed ghettos. A rising birth rate among Catholics brought the nationalist population to more than 40 percent of the whole and though successful attempts were made at integrated education, they were non-significant statistically. Some of the changes were quite remarkable. Who could have foretold that Alex Maskey (1952–), a well-known Republican, would have been elected Lord Mayor of Belfast in 2002, or that Anne Brolly would become Sinn Féin mayor of the plantation town of Limavady, County Derry that now had a nationalist majority within the town boundaries in 2003. Derry city had had a system of electing mayors from different parties from the time of the city council's restoration in 1973 but here the polarisation was most apparent: a large majority of Unionists, even those of the middle classes, had over the years moved house to the Waterside part of the city, on the east bank of the Foyle.

In the 1990s Unionists, acutely conscious of a perceived diminution of their hegemony, turned as if for comfort to the old pieties of Orangeism and its associated brotherhoods, such as the Royal Black Institution and the Apprentice Boys of Derry. The 'marching season' had been a part of the North's summer for more than a hundred years. The routes of these 'walks', as they call them, have long been jealously preserved as part of the orders' unyielding traditions. But what may once have been innocuous pathways now lay through built-up areas. Some Derry nationalists objected to the Apprentice Boys' circuit of the walls in celebration of the city's seventeenth-century siege. In the past when the 'walkers' passed that part of the circuit that overlooked the nationalist Bogside they tended to insult the inhabitants by throwing coins, to be met by deliberately smoky chimneys. It was some such actions on 12 August 1969 that sparked the violence that led to such seismic changes in Northern Ireland. The Bogside Residents Association worked for years in the late 1990s to achieve a compromise that would allow the walk without offending the people who lived below the walls. The Apprentice Boys' days – 18 December to celebrate the closing of the gates against the Jacobites and 12 August to commemorate the relief of the city – had become occasions for serious rioting. Recent years have seen a reasonable accommodation, which allows that part of Protestant tradition, which they regard as essential, to be enjoyed without offence to the majority population.

The confrontations in Portadown were much more serious. A book written about the series of stand-offs had the subtitle, 'The Orange Order's Last Stand'. This is something of an exaggeration but there *were* battle lines drawn. The green hill that led down to the Garvaghy Road became the twentieth-century equivalent of the 'green grassy slopes of the Boyne', in the words of the ballad that commemorated William III's victory over James II at Oldbridge, County Meath on 1 July 1690 (old calendar). The traditional walk was held on the Sunday before 12 July, the anniversary of the Boyne battle. The Portadown lodges marched to Drumcree Church and after a religious service they returned by the Garvaghy Road. This was fine when that road was a country lane but by the 1990s it led though a densely populated nationalist housing estate. The changed situation made no impression on the tradition-fixated Orangemen. They regarded their route as sacrosanct and seemed to be unaware of the effect their banners, drums and arrogant mien had on people who did not share their culture. The return march was always contentious but trouble did not begin until 9 July 1995 when they were prevented from going down the road because that part of the day's proceedings had been banned. During the stand-off the crowd was addressed by Paisley and David Trimble (1944–), the local MP and a law lecturer at Queen's University, Belfast. After some rioting there and in Unionist areas, with roads to the port of Larne blocked, an uneasy compromise was reached. The marchers were allowed to proceed silently down the road after agreeing not to walk there again in coming years. Though Trimble denied this all the mediators insisted that the end of the Garvaghy Road part of the walk had been agreed. Paisley and Trimble, not natural allies, were seen on television apparently skipping triumphantly down to the RUC barrier.

During the year attempts were made to prevent a reoccurrence of the now menacing stand-off but to no avail. The march was banned again and the road blocked by the RUC on 7 July 1996. There followed some of the worst civil disturbances in Protestant areas and elsewhere that the North had seen since the UWC stoppage. Roads were blocked, cars hijacked and set on fire, and breezeblocks dropped from bridges on to the M1 motorway. The fire service reported its busiest period for twenty-five years. The Craigavon Bridge in Derry was blocked by a crowd including Richard Dallas, the city's Unionist mayor, who was later removed from office. The death of a Catholic taxi driver, Michael McGoldrick, shot by Protestant paramilitaries, was blamed on the murderous rhetoric of some of the Unionist speeches. On 11 July Sir Hugh Annesley, the RUC Chief Constable, rescinded his ban and the Orangemen were forced down the road. The result was fierce rioting in nationalist areas. In 1997 the army and the RUC sealed off the road, allowing the marches to move silently down the road where, as well as in other nationalist areas, there was later rioting. In the thirty-six hours afterwards there were 548 attacks on the security forces, 691 petrol bombings, and fifteen gun and bomb assaults on the RUC.

A Parades Commission, set up in March 1997 to determine whether contentious parades should take place, demanded that the 1998 Garvaghy Road march be re-routed. Army engineers set up a steel barrier and a kind of medieval moat to prevent access. There was another stand-off with fierce violence while exhausted police and soldiers bore the brunt of Protestant attacks. The deaths of three Catholic children in Ballymoney after a loyalist arson attack were blamed on heightened emotions over Drumcree; revulsion at the act caused many protesters to leave the scene. The problem of Drumcree and the Garvaghy Road remains unresolved. Some believe that the adamantine insistence on rights by the Portadown Orangemen brings the reputation of the Order into even greater dispute and millions of pounds have been spent each year carrying out the Parades Commission's instructions. Since 2001 the event has been quieter and less inflammatory but the behaviour of the RUC in batoning a path for the marches in 1997 scattered the last fragment of acceptability of that force in the Catholic community. Even with radical reforms implemented after the Patten Report (1999) the residual suspicion of a solely Northern Ireland police service remained as strong a stumbling block on the weary road to peace as arms decommissioning.

In spite of the yearly tensions at Drumcree the Peace Process limped on. Its character was rather that of an iceberg with most of the volume beneath the surface or, to change the metaphor, like the beautiful glide of a swan while the frantic motion of busy legs is unseen. The Labour landslide of 1997 swept it on. Tony Blair had such a majority that he had no need to depend on Unionist members, and already he had formed an ambition to seek the final solution of the centuries-old Irish Question. His joint announcement with Mo Mowlam on 30 January 1998 of the setting up of the Saville tribunal into Bloody Sunday greatly increased nationalist confidence in the new regime. This was one of the positive results of a new PIRA ceasefire that came into force on 20 July 1997.

Most of the political leaders – Trimble now head of official Unionism since the autumn of 1995 (a gift, many believed, of his hardline stance during Drumcree in 1995); Bertie Ahern (1951–), the former Fianna Fáil Finance Minister, who became Taoiseach on 26 June; Blair, ebullient with success after his electoral triumph; and President Clinton – all strove with different velocities to advance the cause of peace. Hume, Adams and Martin McGuinness continued to meet and talk, and George Mitchell was there as a genial chairman, ever ready to charm, admonish and negotiate. His Mitchell principles, adumbrated on 24 January 1996, gave a kind of blueprint for optimum conditions for a working agreement. The most significant 'principle' was that decommissioning should happen in tandem with talks. Blair, whose dynamism was in noted contrast to Major's four years of dithering, set 15 September as the date for inclusive talks, with May 1998 as the deadline for agreement. He also announced the setting-up of an international body to supervise the decommissioning of Republican and Loyalist arms under the chairmanship of the Canadian general, John de Chastelain (1937–). It was Mitchell who nominated 9 April 1998 – Holy Thursday – as the final date. In fact when the Belfast Agreement was finally signed it was five o'clock on Good Friday, giving the accord its popular name.

The work towards that happy conclusion was tedious, laborious and made the mills of God seem to move at hyperspeed. For a start Paisley and his DUP, soon to become the largest parliamentary party, walked out of the conference and one UUP member, Jeffrey Donaldson, after bitter criticism of his party over the 'concessions' envisaged by the agreement, eventually crossed the floor to join the DUP. Fissures began to show in the PIRA as well. After a meeting in Gweedore, County Donegal, a breakaway group was formed assuming the mantle of the 'Real IRA'(also known as Óglaigh na hÉireann), and joined the 'Continuity' IRA in carrying on the 'armed struggle'. The most notorious of their actions was the Omagh bombing of 15 August 1998. Considering the objections and the rejections and the cajoling required, one still wonders how the agreement was reached.

A bare majority of Unionists accepted it, largely due to the unexpectedly conciliatory attitude of Trimble and such unlikely people as David Ervine (1954–2007), who as leader of the Progressive Unionist Party (PUP) had helped negotiate the UVF ceasefire, and Billy Hutchinson, also of the PUP. When the agreement was accepted and the countrywide referendum held on 22 May confirmed this, the sense of satisfaction was profound. There was an 81 percent poll (the second highest in the history of Northern Ireland) with a 71.1 percent approval rate, and in the South a 56 percent poll produced 94.4 percent in favour of the agreement and supporting changes to those Articles of the Irish constitution which concerned the Republic's claim to sovereignty over the whole island.

The talks agenda had three strands, giving rise to much wordplay, such as 'shifting strands' and the 'riddle of the strands', a pun on the title of the famous adventure novel by Erskine Childers (1870–1922). Strand One dealt with democratic institutions in Northern Ireland and proposed the establishment of a 108-member assembly that would have positions assigned on the basis of party strength. Strand Two set up a North/South ministerial council, and the third strand, the least controversial of all, dealt with relations between the sovereign governments, including the devolved institutions of Northern Ireland, Scotland and Wales. The accelerated release of 'political' prisoners was promised and Chris Patten (1944–), former governor of Hong Kong, was appointed chairman of an Independent Commission on Policing. Decommissioning of arms by paramilitaries was required and Sinn Féin was urged to take up its full role in devolved governmental committees, including membership of the Policing Board. The police issue and that of the decommissioning of arms were to remain as the sticking points for both sides. Over the next nine years there were to be many go-slows and sometimes grinding halts. Blair and Ahern continued the frustrating and enervating work of peacemaking, issuing a number of 'absolutely final' threats to abandon the whole idea of a devolved assembly and revert to permanent direct rule, such as the other Celtic fringe territories that England had acquired during the centuries had enjoyed or suffered before the setting up of parliaments in Cardiff and Edinburgh.

The two main obstacles to the progress of peace were the PIRA's attitude to decommissioning and relations with the new Police Service of Northern Ireland (PSNI), which had replaced the unacceptable RUC, and the clear reluctance on the part of Unionists to believe that the PIRA could be trusted finally to put their armaments beyond use and, by spurning all criminal activities fully, to accept the law of the land. At first, in spite of the vocal opposition of many Unionists, especially the DUP who had refused to accept the Good Friday Agreement, visible advances were made. A legislative assembly with extensive devolved powers was finally in session on 2 December 1999 with Trimble as first minister and Seamus Mallon (1936–), MP for Newry and Armagh and deputy leader of the SDLP, as his deputy. The assembly speaker was John – later Lord – Alderdice of Knock (1955–). Mallon had once described the Good Friday Agreement as 'Sunningdale for slow learners', an admonition directed at both extremes of the political divide. Elections were to be held on May Day every five years and the assembly holding ministerial appointments in proportion to the number of seats held by each party.

Devolved powers included Education, Health, Agriculture, Transport and Culture. Not included in the list were Criminal Law and Police. The force, after Patten's reforms, looked different; the old green militaristic uniform became black and was softened. The members of the force were as likely to appear in baseball caps as in peaked headgear, with open-necked shirts. Recruitment was intended to remedy the population imbalance in the police force with a 93 percent Protestant membership in a society which now is 43 percent Catholic. Sinn Féin's refusal to recognise the force until January 2007 and to have its members cooperate delayed the achievement of Patten's recommended 50 percent of each. Recruitment of nationalists, after formal encouragement by Gerry Adams, started to increase. A Police Ombudsman, Nuala O'Loan (1951–), an English-born solicitor and law lecturer, was appointed in 1998 and proved popular with the general acceptance of all but a few in her rulings. On 22 January 2007 she established proof after her investigation, with the codename 'Operation Ballast', of collusion between the UDA and the Special Branch in the killing of certain individuals including Raymond McCord Jr, whose father Raymond campaigned for ten years to have his son's death investigated. Confidence in the PSNI increased with the appointment as chief constable of Sir Hugh Orde (1959–) on 29 May 2002. A man of quiet charisma, Orde strove to remove from the force any suggestion of partiality, a task that continued under the reign of his successor, Matt Baggott.

The assembly faltered four times: suspended from 11 February to 30 May 2000, on 10 August and 22 September in 2001, each time for twenty-four hours, and on 14 October 2002 *sine die*. Each time it was Trimble who made the decision, threatening to abandon the assembly and finally doing so. His reasons were the perceived illegal actions of the PIRA or their inadequate response to the required demand for decommissioning. This was finally seen to be done in September 2005 when de Chastelain, as chairman of the decommissioning body, persuaded the British and Irish governments that the PIRA had put all their weapons beyond use and had disposed of its explosives. Under the careful anxious tutelage of Adams, McGuinness and other Sinn Féin leaders, the cry in the Republican areas of 'Not a single bullet, not a single ounce [of Semtex]' had become obsolete. With a reassuring report from the International Monitoring Commission on 30 January 2007 that criminality had virtually ceased Tony Blair and Bertie Ahern were able to announce that elections for the assembly would indeed take place – as planned under the terms of the St Andrews' Agreement on Friday, 13 October 2006 – on 7 March 2007 with the first meeting of a new power-sharing assembly on 26 March.

12

Peace and Power-sharing

IN SEAN O'CASEY'S PLAY *THE SHADOW of a Gunman*, the character of the pedlar, Seamus Shields, repeats as a kind of mantra the line, 'O Kathleen ni Houlihan, your way's a thorny way!' The line is a slight misquotation from the poem, 'The Passing of the Gael' by Ethna Carbery (1866–1902) that had a great vogue at the time. Though the play was first presented in 1923 the line is still applicable to Northern Ireland's search for not exactly peace – it has a kind of a working lack of violence – but for the structures that will ease sectarian tensions and create a long-lasting amity. From the prospect of the 1970s or even the 1980s such non-violence would have seemed an unbelievable achievement but wishes answered always create further wishes. Intervening elections showed a weakening of middle ground parties and growth of strength for the DUP and Sinn Féin. The DUP gained nine seats in the 2005 UK general election, while Sinn Féin became the largest nationalist party, winning six seats, including one originally held by Seamus Mallon of the SDLP. He had by then retired from politics following his leader John Hume, who resigned in September 2001 for health reasons. Sinn Féin, no longer an abstentionist party, also won five seats in the 2002 Dáil election and had increased this to a remarkable tally of fourteen by 2011. Its polar opposite, the DUP, always referred to the party as 'Sinn Féin/IRA' and one of the causes for the snail's pace of political progress was the DUP's suspicion of its strong links with paramilitaries.

The belief that paramilitaries on both sides had drifted into criminality was not without foundation. Some of its members were confidently believed to be involved in petrol and cigarette smuggling, in drugs, protection rackets involving building sites (of which there were many because of more than thirty years of bombing and necessary slum clearances), and severe punishment shootings and beatings. It was hard for people to believe that 'the war was over' when, on a raid on the Northern Bank headquarters in Belfast on Sunday, 19 December 2004, £26 million was stolen, presumably by the PIRA. New notes were printed almost immediately allowing Hugh Orde to dismiss the raid as winning no more for the perpetrators than a 'lot of waste paper'. Sinn Féin insisted that the robbery was not authorised, indicating that there were some independent elements in the PIRA that were becoming uncontrollable. Six weeks later, on 30 January 2005, after a fight in Magennis's pub in May Street in Belfast city centre, Robert McCartney was stabbed to death, it was alleged, by members of the PIRA. His fiancee and sisters demanded that the PIRA admit the killing and, bizarrely, in March the PIRA offered to kill the killers. The McCartneys, who lived in the nationalist Short Strand area, claimed in October 2005 that they had been intimidated out of their homes from the district where the family had lived for five generations.

It is believed that the shadow of the bank raid and McCartney's death had some effect on the voting in May when it was felt that Sinn Féin might have done even better and more or less obliterated the SDLP as the DUP had the UUP, who won only a single seat in the middle class constituency of North Down when Sylvia Hermon was elected. The SDLP had lost its two charismatic leaders – Hume, who had shared the Nobel Prize for Peace with Trimble in 1988, and Mallon, who had been second minister in the assembly. Its support was seen to be aging and perhaps a bit bourgeois, though in fact it had many working class voters. Hume's successor as leader of the party, Mark Durkan (1960–), was vigorous and bright but was not as well known, and had not had the same media exposure as his predecessors.

The assembly while it lasted had shown an expectedly more precise orientation to Northern Ireland affairs than the NIO and had made some bold moves supported, at least temporarily, by an indulgent Treasury. Free travel was given to the over sixty-fives and as in the South had more than paid for itself by improved wellbeing and lower health costs in that vulnerable age group. On 1 April 2010, free prescriptions were introduced by the Health Minister, Michael McGimpsey. A serious traffic bottleneck at Toomebridge, County Antrim, was greatly eased by the building of an elegant bridge over the Lower Bann, and Martin McGuinness, whilst Minister of Education, set in motion a controversial process by which the transfer system to secondary schools, known as the Eleven Plus, seen by some as educationally undesirable, might be replaced and change the character of secondary grammar schools.

Rule by Irishmen concerned with local affairs seemed preferable to that of the NIO and a series of secretaries of state whose interest and even loyalties might seem to be divided. Peter Mandelson (1953–) who replaced Mo Mowlam in October 1999 was more popular with Unionists than his predecessor but had to relinquish the post the following January. He was followed by John Reid (1947–) who stayed until October 2002 and Paul Murphy (1948–) who left in May 2005. His replacement was Peter Hain (1950–) who was also secretary for Wales, the shared responsibility seen as a derogation of Northern Ireland's importance. After the Conservatives regained control (in a coalition government with the Liberal Democrats) at Westminster in 2010, Owen Paterson was appointed as Northern Secretary.

The idea of power, however limited and controlled, being in the hands of Sinn Féin was unacceptable to many Unionists but for a while the system seemed to work. Tony Blair's ambition to achieve a settlement in Northern Ireland seemed tantalisingly near but a perceived dilatoriness on Sinn Féin's part in the business of the decommissioning of arms and decriminalisation of its associated paramilitaries proved too much. The manifest advantage at least in the short term of local as opposed to Westminster's slightly distracted rule was not enough to persuade the DUP, now the largest Unionist party, to look with other than deep suspicion at Sinn Féin, the largest nationalist party and with whom they had to cooperate in the running of Northern Ireland. The prospect of sharing power with 'ex-terrorists' was not to be thought of without radical reform.

Some shifts by Sinn Féin, as we have seen, removed the stated impediments but the DUP seemed still not to be satisfied, asking for actions not words. One of the reasons for the thorny way's delay on the Republican side was the need for persuasion that the war was really over not so much for their opponents as for their own side. The 'armed struggle' that had caused so much grief and pain had for some members not achieved its continually asserted purpose – the reunification of Ireland. What the Belfast and St Andrews' agreements had achieved seemed no more than a reaffirmation of partition, whatever about its safeguards for the minority and the proliferation of cross-border initiatives.

The political situation in Northern Ireland became like a distorted mirror image of the South after the Treaty, with many disaffected entities in need of assuagement. A large majority of Republicans now seem ready to follow the advice and admonitions of the Sinn Féin leaders. After recent serious crimes they have been urged to bring what information they have to the PSNI, an index of a remarkable change of policy. There are dissidents, of course, but they are probably a small minority and, despite random but occasionally deadly attacks and sporadic bomb scares, are perhaps as ineffectual as the Republican rump that opposed de Valera's formation of the Fianna Fáil party in 1926 and its ruling of the country from 1932 until 1948. After months and years of necessary slow progress Sinn Féin seems to have removed obstacles, internal and external, and to have lent some support to McGuinness's claim that Sinn Féin will in a generation be the majority party in Northern Ireland and achieve at last its destiny. The internal difficulties of the DUP and to a lesser extent the UUP have also to be faced. Tergiversation is extremely difficult for people encouraged to be adamant. The leaders of the DUP face a kind of equivalent need for the reassurance of its followers that Sinn Féin seems to have managed on its side.

Local elections now have an entirely new character, and slogans that were effective in the past are no longer relevant. Kathleen ni Houlihan's thorny way may prove smoother but since nothing works out as expected in Northern Ireland it may be afflicted with unexpected new thorns. The history of Northern Ireland's existence since its unfortunate birth gives even the sanguine little confidence about settlement. Sectarian tensions have not diminished and one can understand the Unionist certainty that their political position has been steadily eroded. The confident, not to say triumphalist, feeling that their Ulster (if no one else's) that promised so well at its inception and continued so well – with British help – could survive in the form that they wished has been dissipated and they are bitterly conscious of their displacement from top positions of power. A majority does not relish the prospect of sharing power with their former bitter enemies. They still have, however, the satisfaction that reunification seems as far away as ever, that Stormont rule, though fundamentally different from its nature in the past, is now on a firmer basis. Unionism no longer has an impenetrable and unshakable majority but has fewer disaffected in the steadily growing minority.

The new regime, if all the parties agree to work it, makes the prospect of a united Ireland ever more unlikely. The Welsh Wizard's conjuring trick did not in fact work. It is this that provides the motivation for the activities of the several dissident Republican groups who find it difficult to follow Sinn Féin's wary acceptance of the PSNI and willingness to share power in a system that apparently copper-fastens partition; this difficulty is reflected in the presence at election times of candidates who run on an anti-PSNI, anti-agreement, and anti-Sinn Féin leadership ticket. Some of their opposite numbers, however, have issues with the agreements of 1998 and 2006, regarding them as a sell-out and gross betrayal, leading to former DUP supporters standing in opposition to official candidates and the formation of such political groupings as Traditional Unionist Voice (TUV) who, as quoted from their website, 'reject unrepentant terrorists at the heart of government' and aim 'to keep the brake on DUP concessions'.[1]

As I have suggested in Chapter One, fully to understand the North requires some knowledge of the ancient province of Ulster and its seventeenth-century plantations. The Irish as a nation – Ulster being no exception – are accused of being obsessed by history.[2] The truth is that the Irish know very little history but are imbued from childhood with much visceral propaganda. As one surveys the Northern Ireland state from its inglorious beginnings and generally inept political story it remains inexplicable unless it is realised that the several seventeenth-century plantations that were intended to render the northern province 'civil' worked and didn't work.

They worked in that the hard-working immigrants, especially those from the border shires of Scotland, took the apparent concomitant wildness that made Ulster more Gaelic and essentially older in its structure and culture than the other provinces and tried to replicate the order and patterns of their original homeland. Their dismissal of the native Ulster people as 'woodkernes', while inevitable, did neither party justice. Two vastly different ideologies with two irreconcilable cultures clashed and are still patently at odds. The plantation policy failed in that the leaderless natives could not be extirpated as had been done in Virginia in the New World – stories of the savagery in both colonies were identical. They survived trailing ancestral dreams of a lost possession. They kept to the old religion, a dangerous practice in the seventeenth century when reformation meant a quick way with heretics. Most deleterious of all, their labour, as tenants-at-will, was necessary if 'civility' were properly to be established.

Two great seventeenth-century 'what ifs' remain to tease us in what is rarely anything more than a sophisticated parlour game: what if Hugh O'Neill had stayed and won in Ulster the battle he lost at Kinsale? And what if Phelim O'Neill had not risen in 1641? The results of those two decisions are with us still. The two cloths of Ulster Protestantism and Ulster Catholicism could never through the centuries be successfully sewn together. As in the Biblical parable you cannot patch old cloth with new. This dangerous otherness was constant and grew steadily more perilous as penal legislation was relaxed and Catholics began to play a significant part in society. The mentality that showed itself in the construction of seventeenth-century bawns, those forts of defence against the dispossessed, persisted. The various orders dedicated to glorious, pious and immortal memories revert to old hatreds under threat while, on the other side, in Yeats's words, 'Too long a sacrifice can make a stone of the heart.' The mixture of fear and despisal is the most potent cause of violence and brutality on both sides. Most people, not just the war-weary, long with a passion for peace but it must be a genuine peace based on respect and understanding.

After more than forty years of life in the fissile North it is hard for people over fifty to be optimistic. The most sanguine hope for the best but cannot help being somewhat fearful for the worst. Living in the state created by the Welsh Wizard's botched trick has prevented its inhabitants from forming any coherent idea of the political future. For both sides lost certainties have had to be replaced by the will to prevent a recurrence of the nightmare that they survived. If progress can continue to be made, the earned euphoria of the absence of violence will increasingly be tempered by economic reality and other considerations, such as global warming, will have to assume equal rank with old dreams of a united Ireland or a restoration of Unionist supremacy. Perhaps, too, the 'dreary spires' of Churchill's famous speech will not emerge again as a bane nor the integrity of their ancient quarrel remain as absolute as in the past. Now at last it may be that all the old fears are being laid bare and confronted and old historical certainties shown to be hollow; might there be some expectancy of rapprochement? In Seamus Heaney's words from his play, *The Cure at Troy* (1990), might hope and history at last rhyme?

NOTES, SELECT BIBLIOGRAPHY AND INDEX

NOTES ON THE TEXT

Chapter One

[1]Winston Churchill, his colleague, is credited with originating the even more trigger-happy 'Auxies' – the Auxiliary Division of the Royal Irish Constabulary (RIC) – the blue-uniformed ex-officers, infamous for burning Balbriggan and Cork in 1920 and for turning their guns on the spectators in Croke Park on 'Bloody Sunday' on 11 December 1920.

[2]Northern intransigence was also a contributory factor.

[3]The Apprentice Boys society had been founded in 1814, analogous to the Orange Order, and named after the thirteen London apprentices who had symbolically shut the ferry quay gate against the Jacobite troops of Lord Antrim in December 1688. They parade twice each year wearing 'Derry crimson' collarettes in memory of the bloody flag that flew there during the siege.

[4]The precipitate ending of PR by Dawson Bates (1876–1949), the new Minister of Home Affairs, in 1922 gave Derry Unionist mayors until 1968 when responsibility for civic matters was taken over by an appointed commission.

Chapter Two

[1]The Russian pogroms were motivated by sectarianism, anti-Semitism not being approved by Russian orthodoxy, and carried out by the Russian army.

[2]Duodecimo is the smallest size of book page and Demosthenes, who lived 384–322 BC, was the greatest of the Athenian orators.

[3]This tactic he would use again when Sir Richard Dawson Bates, his flinty Minister for Home Affairs, made one of his first acts in cabinet to abolish the PR system of voting for local government elections, one of the safeguards promised to Catholics.

Chapter Three

[1]Glengall Street was the location of the Ulster Unionist Party headquarters.

Chapter Five

[1]That number had been increased to 243 by 1942.

Chapter Six

[1]The Act had been tabled at Stormont at the same time but a kind of Unionist Fabianism delayed for three years.

[2]The word 'notable' used in the statement was one that might interest lawyers and confuse the priest in the confessional.

Chapter Seven

[1] One might say that the tricolour acted for Paisley as a red rag to a bull, except that the metaphor seems mixed.

[2] Coincidentally, though it reads like bad theatre, the police officer who escorted Currie out of the house was her brother.

[3] The Cameron Commission set up by O'Neill in January 1969 to inquire into the events of the day found that the Apprentice Boys had no such tradition.

Chapter Eight

[1] They called themselves 'provisional' intending to obtain ratification at a convention in 1970. The origin of the nickname 'Stickies' is lost in obscurity; one given explanation is that their Easter lilies worn to commemorate the 1916 rising were adhesive rather than pinned.

[2] The Social Democratic and Labour Party had been founded on 21 August the previous year with Gerry Fitt and John Hume at its head.

Chapter Twelve

[1] In spite of such opposition, the DUP and Sinn Féin still re-emerged after the May 2011 assembly elections as the two most dominant parties with the most votes and hence the most seats.

[2] James Joyce's character, Stephen Dedalus, the Telemachus of *Ulysses*, said history was a nightmare from which he was trying to awake.

Select Bibliography

Abbott, Richard. *Police Casualties in Ireland, 1919–1922*. Cork: 2000

Bardon, Jonathan. *A History of Ulster*. Belfast: 1992

Bew, Paul & Gillespie, Gordon. *Northern Ireland: A Chronology of the Troubles 1968–1999*. Dublin: 1999

Buckland, Patrick. *James Craig, Lord Craigavon*. Dublin: 1980

—————————. *A History of Northern Ireland*. Dublin: 1981

Clarke, Howard (ed). *Irish Cities*. Cork: 1995

Connolly, S J. (ed). *The Oxford Companion to Irish History*. Oxford: 1998

Elliott, Marianne. *The Catholics of Ulster*. London: 2000

Elliott, Sydney & Flackes, W D. *Northern Ireland: A Political Directory 1968–1999*. Belfast: 1999

Feeney, Brian. *A Pocket History of the Troubles*. Dublin: 2004

Ferriter, Diarmaid. *The Transformation of Ireland 1900–2000*. London: 2004

Fisk, Robert. *In Time of War*. London: 1985

Foster, R F. *Modern Ireland 1600–1972*. London: 1988

Gallagher, Ronan. *Violence and Nationalist Politics in Derry City, 1920–1923*. Dublin: 2003

Harkness, David. *Northern Ireland since 1920*. Dublin: 1983

Hennessy, Thomas. *A History of Northern Ireland, 1920–1996*. Dublin: 1997

—————————. *The Northern Ireland Peace Process: Ending the Troubles?* Dublin: 2000

Lacey, Brian. *Siege City – The Story of Derry and Londonderry*. Belfast: 1990

Lyons, F S L. *Ireland since the Famine*. London: 1971

Mc Gladdery, Gary. *The PIRA in England: The Bombing Campaign 1973–1997*. Dublin: 2006

McKittrick, David & McVea, David. *Making Sense of the Troubles*. Belfast: 2000

Murphy, Desmond. *Derry, Donegal and Modern Ulster 1790–1921*. Derry: 1981

Murray, Gerard & Tonge, Jonathan. *Sinn Féin and the SDLP*. Dublin: 2005

O'Clery, Conor. *Phrases Make History Here*. Dublin: 1986

O'Connor, Fionnuala. *Breaking the Bonds: Making Peace in Northern Ireland*. Edinburgh: 2002

Ryder, Chris & Kearney, Vincent. *Drumcree: The Orange Order's Last Stand*. London: 2001

Stewart, A T Q. *The Ulster Crisis 1912–1914*. London: 1967

——————. *Edward Carson*. Dublin: 1981

Wichert, Sabine. *Northern Ireland since 1945*. London: 1991

Index